MARLENE
Portraits 1926–1960
DIETRICH

With an Introduction
by Klaus-Jürgen Sembach
and an Epilogue
by Josef von Sternberg

Translation
by Arthur S. Wensinger
and Richard H. Wood

Schirmer/Mosel · Grove

ACKNOWLEDGMENTS

The plans for this book could never have materialized without the generous support, the friendly cooperation, and the substantial commitment of many people and many institutions. The publishers gratefully acknowledge all the contributing photographers, their agents or the administrators of their estates, as well as the many individuals in charge of various archives, museums, photo agencies, and photography collections who helped us procure the illustrations for this volume.

In particular we thank Horst P. Horst, New York, for his helpful encouragement during the earliest stages of our work, as well as John Kobal and Simon Crocker of the Kobal Collection, London, who most generously placed its treasures at our disposal and thereby made it possible for us to produce this book in its present form.

Our gratitude is also extended to Meri von Sternberg, Los Angeles; Hans Helmut Prinzler and Peter Magdowski of the Stiftung Deutscher Kinemathek, Berlin; Professor Klaus Honnef of the Rheinisches Landesmuseum, Bonn; Dr. Reinhold Misselbeck of the Museum Ludwig, Cologne; Dr. Paul Naredi-Rainer of the Rheinisches Bildarchiv, Cologne; Helgard Repp-Gulow of the STERN Syndicate, Hamburg; Helga Margret Colle-Tiz, Angelica Blechschmidt, and Angelika Schreier of VOGUE Deutschland, Munich; Leslie Pell van Breen of Sotheby's Belgravia, London; Anton Bruehl, Jr., San Francisco; Shelley Dowell of the Richard Avedon Studio, New York; Barbara Puorro-Galasso of the George Eastman House, Rochester, New York; Ned Leavitt and Sheila O'Shea of the William Morris Agency, New York; Mary Corliss of the Museum of Modern Art, New York; Anne-Marie Perier of the Editions Filipacchi, Paris; Pat McCabe, New York; Ulrich Kurowski, Munich; Michael Meyring, New York; Reinhard Selzer, Munich; Monika Faber, Vienna; Renate Seydel of the Henschel Verlag, Berlin, German Democratic Republic.

The translators wish to acknowledge the invaluable assistance of Jeanine Basinger and Joseph W. Reed, Jr., and the persistent spirit of Bolly Hassan.

The Epilogue »The Making of Marlene« is reprinted from *Fun in a Chinese Laundry*
by Josef Sternberg, © 1965 by Josef von Sternberg, by permission of Meri von Sternberg,
Los Angeles.

Copyright © 1984 by Schirmer/Mosel Munich
All Rights Reserved
No part of this book may be reproduced, stored in a retrieval system, or transmitted in any form,
by any means, including mechanical, electronic, photocopying, recording, or otherwise,
without the prior written permission of the publisher.

ISBN: 0-394-54264-9
Library of Congress Catalog Card Number: 84-51370
Manufactured in West Germany

Distributed by Grove Press, Inc.
196 West Houston Street
New York, N.Y. 10014

THE PHOTOGRAPHERS

Kenneth Alexander
Richard Avedon
Cecil Beaton
Erwin Blumenfeld
Davis Boulton
Anton Bruehl
Mario von Bukovich
Irving Chidnoff
Harry Croner
Alfred Eisenstaedt
Don English
John Engstead
Ed Estabrook
François Gragnon
Milton H. Greene
W. von Gudenberg
Horst P. Horst
George Hoyningen-Huene
George Hurrell
Ray Jones
Herbert List

Harald Meisert
Nikolas Muray
d'Ora
Norman Parkinson
Irving Penn
Ted Reed
Eugene R. Richee
A. L. 'Whitey' Schaefer
Lord Snowdon
Edward Steichen
Liselotte Strelow
Turnbridge
William Walling, Jr.
Scotty Welbourne
Laszlo Willinger

CONTENTS

9

Klaus-Jürgen Sembach
The Well-Wrought Illusion
(translated by Arthur S. Wensinger
and Richard H. Wood)

31

The Plates

249

Josef von Sternberg
The Making of Marlene

269

Photo Credits

THE WELL-WROUGHT ILLUSION

Every star is an industrial product. Widespread public recognition, the prerequisite for stardom, has become possible only through the achievements of modern technological reproduction, and without film and television the present-day idol would be unthinkable. Nor is it the product's dissemination alone that is an industrial process. The same can also be said for its manufacture, which represents a similar kind of technological application – although, to be sure, it cannot be accomplished without specific contributions from the individual involved. The critical point is the extent to which personality can be sustained under these frankly impersonal conditions.

Such might constitute a rough outline for an approach to the consideration of stardom. There are idols, coldly synthesized in test-tubes, whose impacts are short-lived and artificial. Behind the poses of others, the human dimension shines forth, and as a rule these endure longer. They allow for closer examination, and their fabricated exteriors do not completely obscure the existence of the human soul. These, in short, are the true stars – those beings who personifiy ideal images for the »I« of the spectator.

Adoration presumably perceives this process rather differently – less soberly, less rationally – but be that as it may, behind it all lies a calculating intention whose aim is success and nothing else, and which time and time again has proven itself merciless. If it is to have any real chance for success, the product must be appropriately conceived and accurately designed, and one of the elementary prerequisites for a successful product is to establish a feeling for its necessity. No single individual can take exclusive charge of this demanding enterprise, and no star has ever been entirely the result of its own solitary efforts; from the beginning, it has been a joint creation of the many. The star process is set in motion by the discoverer and it ends with the dedicated offices of the person who applies a final layer of face powder. Everyone in between gets to put in a word and thus to transform the original discovery, and nothing of significance transpires without those manipulations whose desired goal is the metamorphosis of promising material into a kind of super-configuration. The individual *per se* is never enough. Only a process of deliberate and perceptive stylization is adequate to the task of attracting broad public interest.

Once an image has been created, attempts at changing it have nearly always been disastrous. Shifts from one specialized design to another (and, in conjunction with that, major remodelings of appearances) have rarely been accepted, and it is evident that they are taken as offenses against the established order of things. Stars who cherish impossible notions of »change« merely reveal their own ignorance of the very foundations of their existence. The wise ones among the gods are those who remain unalterable, unequivocal, statuesque. Even though they may inwardly rebel, they recognize the obligations and restrictions of what it is that they embody; and the gift they receive in return is that modern version of immortality, eternal reappearance in history's repertoire. It is understood that outstanding examples of standards well met shall remain in demand.

The constant need to repeat and reassert one's particular image requires a very special capacity for self-discipline, and stars less firmly fixed in this celestial firmament have come to grief for lack of it – Marilyn Monroe, for example. Others, in contrast, have turned discipline into a kind of driving, religious creed; Joan Crawford and Marlene Dietrich are frequently put forward as two of the true defenders of this virtue, and in the case of the latter, a quality both personal and national has been summoned in evidence – self-control as a manifestation of the Prussian character. This is something that can be admired as enthusiastically in the United States as anywhere else in the world.

THE EXPECTATIONS

I have never met Marlene Dietrich. I know most of her films, but not all. Some of them I have seen many times; certain others I do not regard very highly. Among her songs, I treasure those with the sound of Berlin in them – that is to say, the earlier ones, and also those composed for her later on by emigrant writers. In regard to the photographs, I believe that I know my way around pretty well. Still shots have the advantage over the moving image in that they are literally more impressive. Accordingly, one's judgment of them alters less readily, and the evanescence of the cinematic impression can be permanently captured for leisurely perusal in the form of illustrated books. It would be rather foolish, though, to try to play the one against the other. The photographs of Marlene Dietrich are basically offshoots of her film roles; her physiognomy was first formulated there, in the films; and the individual glossy prints are direct reflections of that process. This is true for both the publicity shots made at the various film studios and for the artistic productions of famous photographers. All of them reiterate the archetypal situations on the screen: seduction, triumph, surrender. What they never show, however, is indifference. Marlene Dietrich was never a model in the classic, passive sense, someone who serves essentially as a mere object. On the contrary, she was almost always the determinative actress who makes us realize that the fixed moment, too, is a slice of life, and it is precisely this intensity in her photographs which provides a key to the understanding of our enduring interest in her.

The early photographs of the Berlin period contain only an initial suggestion of this infusion of »personality.« She is still a bit shy, a bit embarrassed, even awkward at times. These very qualities are capable of touching us, certainly, and they are appealing in their reserve, but we cannot overcome the sense that this is a person who is still striving toward fulfillment. The biographical data from these years tend to support this impression. Marlene Dietrich played theater and film roles for nearly a decade without ever receiving the attention which she deserved and which would have provided a decisive impetus to her career. Her appearances were like musical passages which somehow always came to vague and inconclusive endings. Everything requisite to success was present – the beauty of her face, the special allure of her figure (together with appropriate costumes), and the somewhat dire subject matter of the films themselves – but the sparks failed to ignite, time after time. The films were generally successful but they never became Marlene Dietrich films. By the end of the twenties, however, the actress had progressed beyond the occasional supporting role in films whose stars gave her little room for competition, and she had begun to appear in movies that were able to provide her with an independent presence.

One of these was *Eine Frau, nach der man sich sehnt* (American title, *Three Loves*), directed by Kurt Bernhardt (1929). In this film she is the central figure who sets the tragic story in motion and is then unable to control its outcome. The hoped-for elevation of Marlene Dietrich to stardom, in the role of the person who triggers the action and effects changes without herself undergoing any transformation of character, was a specifically intended aspect of this role from its inception, but it did not entirely succeed. The film lacked that ultimate courage to run the risk of becoming a cliché, to attain magnificence through stereotype. Equally ambivalent is Marlene Dietrich's performance, which wavers indecisively between personality and pose without fulfilling either.

Something quite similar had happened to her earlier that same year in *Ich küsse Ihre Hand, Madame (I Kiss Your Hand, Madame)*, a silent film with inserted soundtrack for the songs, directed by the then underrated and since neglected Robert Land. The comic quality of the film is achieved in a rather original way, by persistently demonstrating a kind of intelligent indifference toward itself. It seems to have been made with the left hand, and very deliberately so. Its leading lady, accordingly, proceeds lethargically through the unfolding of a plot which obviously is of no great interest to her. This effect is further enhanced by the off-key portrayal of her lover, a man who behaves more like a father than a paramour and seems fully aware of it. From beginning to end, the consistently false situations complement each other wonderfully, but only for the cognoscenti. The film was hardly a vehicle for spreading

In »Die Frau, nach der man sich sehnt«, (Three Loves), 1929   Photo: Terra

the fame of its actors, and there is something exhausted and run-down about its utter nonchalance.

Nevertheless, the film does anticipate certain behavioral characteristics which were later to prove enormously successful: enticement and seduction brought into play not by vivacity of temperament and other such exertions, but simply through a casual self-assurance of certain victory. All imaginable positions and reactions are pre-set; there is no one on hand who could possibly escape the heroine's net. The mythic presence soon to come is thus already present here in adumbrated form, and the only important thing missing is consistency of style. Another characteristic is present in this film, a hearty, tomboyish quality which was later to become a hallmark of the Marlene Dietrich style throughout her German career. Here, in elegant costume, it was first introduced. The lady would appear to have »arrived,« although in reality that was not yet entirely true.

It is perfectly appropriate for us to ask today why the commitment of such considerable effort to these old films often bore so little fruit. Subsequent successes inevitably show previous attempts to have been »wrong.« They are forced to suffer accusations of missing out on opportunities available to them which were in fact perceived only in retrospect by those clever enough to deduce the reasons success had eluded those earlier ventures. A more fair-minded view of the way things really were would suggest that all of the old ingredients seem to have been the right ones, but that the way in which they were put together had not yet been perfected. »Style« was still obliged to be clear-cut and obvious, and it was subject to a particular set of factors – a typical one, for example, being the predilection of the German film of the twenties for disastrous themes and for portentous exaggerations of real life. And underlying this, to be sure, was a considerable vagueness as to what the film-makers actually wanted to deal with; but this general shortcoming was more than compensated for by the intense way in which their dire material was treated. This approach was simply more useful to their purposes than to permeate the material with subtleties. The expectations of their audience were far better satisfied by the tragical intensification of subject matter than by its realistic presentation. Given the situation, it was virtually impossible for the spectator to step back and take a sober, reflective view. Even by the time the stridently expressionistic phase of German film had run its course, a closely related movement had taken over; it was scarcely different in direction, and it continued to dictate both the choice of thematic material and its treatment. Confronted as they were by the supremacy of grand emotions, attempts at composure and detachment did not stand a chance. Kurt Bernhardt had not sufficiently indulged the prevailing demands, and Robert Land's film was a living contradiction of the reigning style. Audience identification with the protagonist of either of these impertinent experiments was doomed from the start. Marlene Dietrich did indeed attract attention to herself, but she did not become a star.

For a brief moment, it seemed that fulfillment was at hand. The director Georg Wilhelm Papst was prepared to give Marlene Dietrich the role of Lulu in his film version of Frank Wedekind's tragedy,

At the Berlin Journalism Ball, 1929
Photo: Alfred Eisenstaedt

In »Morocco«, 1930
Photo: Eugene R. Richee

Pandora's Box (1929). Later, after he had decided on Louise Brooks for the part, he said that Marlene Dietrich would have been »too old and too plain« – at least according to the American actress's memoirs (Louise Brooks, *Lulu in Hollywood,* New York, 1982). Brooks was in fact five years younger, and when we see what she brought to that role it is clear that Papst's decision was the right one. Marlene Dietrich could not have achieved anything even approaching the childlike Lulu; she could never have effected the beautiful unscrupulousness of the New World flapper. And here two careers intersected in a strangely congruent way. Louise Brooks departed Paramount and Hollywood in order to win her real, if short-lived, fame in Europe. Just one year later and at the very same studio that had given away an important piece of its capital, the long-overlooked German actress triumphantly ascended to the position of leading star. Lulu exchanged places with Lola Lola of *The Blue Angel.* They were close relatives, as it were – sisters, almost – but one of them proved to be far more enduring. The Old Continent was to be victorious once again.

The photographs from this period are not particularly revealing. It seems that the complex art of star portraiture was essentially unknown in Germany – indeed, it was perhaps even disdained, a factor in the history of German photography which in itself deserves note. The official studio photos give back to us little more than self-consciousness and embarrassment. The best pictures of Marlene Dietrich were done by photographers who photographed her privately and on their own. Alfred Eisenstaedt appears to have done that frequently during the course of the Berlin film balls, and his picture of her in top hat and tails is probably the most arresting one from this period. Out of the blue, his subject appears here in full regalia, an image so complete, so perfect, that it seems impossible for it ever to have looked otherwise. Pose, costume and expression fit each other exactly, making the apparition immediately plausible. Nothing here is overdone, any awkward touch has been avoided, and perhaps the one thing lacking is a requisite self-assurance of the gaze. In any event, the sudden presence of the subject takes us by surprise. The debut is a success.

THE COSTUME

And it instantly led to further developments: the costume, first of all. Her appropriation of male attire was doubtless a gesture of emancipation, and it suited the image of the times, an image that frequently depicted women in unexpected modes of behavior. Trousers, short hair, lithe and sinewy bodies – all were the outer signs that a transformation of traditional and expected patterns had taken place. The appearance of Marlene Dietrich in men's formal evening clothes was both a provocation and an affirmation – provocative, because with the change in the order of dress, a new androgynous attitude had been launched; affirmative, because it was clear, here and now, that someone had discovered her appropriate sartorial image. The tails were extremely becoming to Marlene Dietrich, and any impression that someone had been subjected to the torments of disguise did not even arise. And so the demonstration ended in a conciliatory way; in the last analysis, it was evident that here was a woman who had conquered with the weapons of her femininity.

Nevertheless, the ultimate impression remained an ambiguous one; the deliberateness of its intention promptly produced the corresponding effect. Josef von Sternberg subsequently exploited it when he introduced Marlene Dietrich to America. That moment in film history is truly breathtaking: it is immediately evident that with the person in top hat and tails who casually strolls onto a stage in a Moroccan honky-tonk bar a new star is born. The moment of the breakthrough can be established to the very second, so to speak. The continuation of the scene is also well known. When a woman in the audience tries to provoke Marlene Dietrich, she kisses her. Thus a further shock follows on the heels of the initial shock of the costume; it dissolves the ambiguity and removes all doubts. Confusion is rampant – but only for a short while. By the time the same props and costume are used again, two years later – in a dance number in

Entertaining U.S. troops in World War II, 1944

the film *Blonde Venus* – a change in color has taken place. Top hat and tails are now white; the negative has been transformed into a positive. But despite this, the actress's hand lightly brushes the tight jersey of one of the »girls« as she dances past. The obligation which is apparently inherent in the transvestite disguise has remained unchanged. But with that, the brilliant effect of the costume seems to have exhausted itself; Marlene Dietrich never again wore top hat and tails in a film. Only decades later, when she returned to the stage, was the costume revived. The effect was the same: a total harmony of costume and personality.

Her outfitting with tail-coat, silk hat, and (as photographs from the Moroccan film reveal) men's shoes basically had the character of a uniform. The classic combination remained exactly as it was supposed to be, not a detail was altered; the wearer assumed without objection the traditionally established garment. It is not known what prompted Marlene Dietrich to dress herself in such a severe and regulated fashion. It is possible that photographs of her father, who died at an early age, inspired her in this. If such was the case, then it is further possible that we are witnesses to the sublimation of an unfulfilled relationship. I suspect, however, that her disciplined nature simply saw itself best reflected in this costume. It was, in point of fact, the very expression of her character. Josef von Sternberg and other directors after him strengthened their leading lady in her inclination to don the uniform, by having her appear as a female cossack or a navy officer, or by putting a shako or other military hat in her hand, which she could then playfully put on and take off. The scene in which she plays a spy in leather military togs has become famous – indeed, infamous. Finally, in the Second World War, she became to all intents and purposes a real soldier and wore the uniform as more than an incidental costume. There are indications – among them the emotional description in her memoirs – that Marlene Dietrich looks back on this time as one of the most important phases of her life.

But even when she gave up outspokenly severe and precise costuming, the details in her manner of dress retained a corresponding severity. The dresses were nearly always buttoned to the neck, close-fitting, and neatly contoured. Neckties, jabots, and pleated ruches replaced the stiff bow tie; jackets and tailored vests took the place of the tails; berets and hats with soft wide brims substituted for the top hat. Boas and other feathered creations often encircled the neck, and little collars were the only adornment to her otherwise convent-like dresses. Strapless gowns were a rarity; shoulders were only reluctantly revealed; and the plunging neckline was all but unknown. Even appearances at her private swimming pool were made under high-buttoned conditions – even though the legs are much in evidence. On the other hand, trousers were always favored, along with anything tightly belted; even corsets, whenever the subject or occasion permitted. Nor should we overlook the laced boots, the classic pumps; but never a hint of those toe-revealing sandals which vulgar colleagues were in the habit of wearing. The famous legs were seldom revealed bare; mostly they were elegantly stockinged – this, too, consistent with the whole style. A »Prussian Style« was in command of all the appointments and it always bespoke discipline and composure. No one has ever seen anything negligent or remiss about Marlene Dietrich's appearance – and anything expressly flattering (furs, for example) served principally to ameliorate the severity.

To return to the early days, however: apart from the tails and silk hat, the clothes she wore during her German period are still without invention or style; they were, in fact, quite homespun. It was not until Travis Banton in Hollywood was put in charge of her wardrobe design that the smart and simple style was achieved which subsequently became its wearer's hallmark. The severe elegance of this wardrobe, with its sacrifice of all accessories, all lively patterns, and whatever else ran the risk of revealing any hint of insecurity, bestowed on Marlene Dietrich the signature of the star which her competition could not so easily approach or emulate. There was, in truth, an unmistakable Marlene Dietrich style. And once it was developed, she never deviated from its classical lines; it was maintained with admirable and remarkable consistency.

THE POSES

The top hat and tails in that photograph by Alfred Eisenstaedt amounted to a proclamation that the not yet established actress Marlene Dietrich had already devised a style for herself. At least the design of her wardrobe now rhymed with the person. In this regard she was almost like the young Chaplin, where the costume seems to have existed even before the role. But the 1929 picture also reveals other things aside from the costume itself. Along with the clothing, there is the appropriate pose: the body just barely leaning against the wall behind, the head at a very slight tilt, *en face*, one hand in a trouser pocket, in the other a cigarette. That is precisely the pose that Josef von Sternberg copied and used in his films several years later. The quiet, gentle, provocative look which asks both what the world costs and whether one is loved. This is me – tell me that it's me. A palpably ambivalent posture can be detected, one which asks for both everything and nothing, and beneath whose suavity lie concealed many personal hurts. After all, this is a woman before us who has had eight years of professional ups and downs.

The cigarette in the hand says just about the same things that the body, the head, and the glance say. It is both assertion and question; naturally a women who wears white tie and tails smokes – but must she really smoke? The language of gesture she speaks with the cigarette has multiple meaning: pleasure, animation, flirtatiousness, and compensation for feelings of insecurity. It is still a bit too early here to make out exactly what is meant, but the harmony between person and prop grows from this point on. There will be whole series of photographs and film scenes in which Marlene Dietrich and the cigarette have a most deliberate and intricate dialogue. She and this object are almost synonymous. And then there is the voice. At first it was still quite high-pitched; later it begins to sound like the voice of a heavy smoker. The cigarette in this key photograph of 1929 has, in brief, an altogether indubitable justification for being there.

What Eisenstaedt did was repeated by nearly all the photographers who followed him. They photographed Marlene Dietrich full-face. Her profile is rarely seen, presumably because of the slight upturn to the nose. *En face,* however, the face is without blemish and (far more often the exception than the rule) seems to be absolutely symmetrical. That by itself would be sufficient reason to explain why photographers have always much preferred taking her full-face.

But there also seem to be other reasons behind this most obvious one; for if one studies portrait series made of other stars, one will eventually notice that *en face* pictures are not the rule. Evidently very few of these subjects have the ability to look the lens – and therefore us – directly in the eye. This observation is startling and somewhat confusing, and it triggers a few doubts and questions in our minds. Has it to do primarily with the cut of these stars' faces, which for the most part are better in profile, or is it that the faces, when they are turned directly at us, tell us too little – even if the features are harmonious? We frequently sense a lack of true participation in these faces, or they betray the strain that comes from trying to look »significant.« Full-face photographs are real visual adventures almost solely in the case of Marlene Dietrich. Direct access to the personality, the intensity of the face that not only is composed but also looks back – these are rarely encountered, but when they are, they do not release the observer readily. These pictures look like invitations to a dialogue: the object is also the subject, and anything but passive.

It is probable that this suggestive effect goes back, along with much else, to Josef von Sternberg's training; but it would have been to no point whatever if the subject had been someone who had nothing from within to contribute. In America, studio portraits of her (which also appropriated the *en-face* technique) became more than the traditional products of the old posing sessions. In a way parallel to the Marlene Dietrich style in clothing, there was now developed a specific style of photographing her. The industry had manufactured a unique new product; not only was it perfect, it was also capable of being »arousing« in a number of different ways.

The eyes, the face, looking out of the picture at us, comprise an essential hallmark whose aura touches us directly. A real sense of closeness arises from these prints which literally transcend their technical medium. The goddess beckons – though presently it would seem more as if she were testing us. The intensity of the photographs with that puzzlingly beautiful face changes over the course of the decades: from the concealed shyness of the early years, to a brief period of artifice and drama, and then to a state of absolute security when the high point of the career is reached in the mid-thirties. After that, the pose tends a bit toward the oracular; in the case of one of the best pictures (taken by Herbert List just before a stage appearance in Germany in 1960), the look is suddenly one of eyes wide, wide open and staring at us. The distance that is normally evoked by the conditions prevailing at a formal photo session is not present in this candid picture. The observer and the observed have reached each other and, so to speak, have consummated the union to which most that had gone before was prelude.

PRUSSIA

It is significant that the moment of this picture occurred in Germany. The relationship of the personality to the place – which by the nature of things she had no choice but to understand was her fatherland – had become in later years a very tense one; perhaps unconsciously it was tense from the very beginning. The lady in white tie and tails must have made a somewhat homeless impression from the start, so ostentatiously did the image renounce all »folksy« attitudes, so clearly did it suggest big-city society – one that went even beyond her ties to Berlin. It was evidently no problem for Marlene Dietrich to trade Germany for the USA and later the USA for France. In 1930 she began her international life, one which became literally worldwide during her tours after the Second World War. What did Germany mean to her in all this?

In no sense did it represent a sentimental foothold for her. We could far sooner say that it constituted a painful aspect of Marlene Dietrich's life. And yet this very fact led to a particularly intense connection between her and the country of her birth – for in my opinion the true patriot is someone who conspicuously suffers the affliction of his or her fatherland. Perhaps that is the only realistic defini-

During her German tour, Munich 1960
Photo: Herbert List

tion of the patriot. At the same time, it is the most unpopular one imaginable; indeed, it stands diametrically opposed to the popular understanding of the term. The young in today's Germany seem increasingly to reject all manifestations of patriotism; perhaps that is the sanest way to get rid of an insoluble problem. What used to be an existential question has become largely self-invalidating, a piece of past history. From this point of view, might we not say that Marlene Dietrich was one of the last German patriots?

Even to ask this question presupposes the acceptance of the definition I propose. Only if patriotism is recognized as »passion« in its most literal sense is there any chance of reaching agreement on this point. Living in the United States was bound to produce in Marlene Dietrich an altogether natural and comprehensible opposition to National Socialist Germany, and her efforts on behalf of the American Army during the War were an expres-

On her German tour, 1960
Photo: Harald Meisert

sion of her feelings. She was performing an act of grief and mourning for the nation to which she belonged by birth.

The German tour of 1960 was no home-coming, but a reassertion of the origins she never disavowed. Herbert List's photograph reveals the tenseness of the event which, along with jubilation and applause, also evoked protest and discord. Her appearance was, after all, not only an artistic but also a political statement. Many were unprepared to forgive the alleged renegade.

The importance of the dowry from the land of her birth is presumably something that Marlene Dietrich is still fully conscious of. The German aspect of her make-up was, in the final analysis, one of the principal factors in the establishment of her fame. It was the specific ingredient that made her unique, since behind all the international style the Prussian officer's daughter remained unmistakable. The way she carried herself, the way she dressed, the way she posed betrayed it, the tautness of her figure, and naturally the blondness of her hair. She was always – even when down on her luck – a women of reserve and bravery.

None of these qualities were altered in any regard – indeed, quite the opposite – when later in her career she entered the world of the Wild West and its saloons. It was precisely here that these virtues must have been most welcome. The particular sort of woman that Marlene Dietrich personified faces the vagaries of life stoically and with composure, of course, but never gives in to fate; she remains active to the end. Even when unmasked as an accomplice, and thus at the end of her rope (that is the way we observe her in Hitchcock's *Stage Fright*, 1950), she nevertheless risks flirting with her guard. The siren goes on singing for as long as humanly possible.

A feeling that the future holds endless possibilities, given the requisite patience and energy, must have been part and parcel of Marlene Dietrich's convictions from the beginning. If not, she would probations from the beginning. If not, she would probably never have had the strength to make so many also a patriot in her line of work, a living repudiation of the assertion, »They never come back.« The successes she had later in life have made Marlene Dietrich clever, insightful and very cautious in the choice of her material. The conviction gained from experience that »things have a way of going on« has prevented her from ever behaving in a confused or over-anxious way. With her, there is no such thing as panic in the final hour, and consequently there are also no premature goodbyes.

POPULARITY AND SUCCESS

When the breakthrough finally came in 1930 with *The Blue Angel*, it was, of all things, with a very German role in a very German film. The disastrous implications inherent in the encounter of the school teacher with the amusing tart in the honky-tonk bar are manifest from the first scene. Outsize, even overdrawn, characters collide here; there is a clashing of extremes – age and youth, brains and legs, helplessness and unscrupulousness, self-pity and mockery. The subtle tones in between are altogether missing, and a cartoon-like exaggeration predominates. All of this made the film immediately accessible to the audience of its day, and it had no problem in entering the mainstream tradition of German screen-melodrama. Its extremely trivial plot was devised in such a way as to render it instantly comprehensible on the simplest level. But the suffocating atmosphere exuded by the fatalistic compression of its material can still be felt today and remains the source of its genuine artistic effect.

The Blue Angel is fundamentally a colossus in a petit-bourgois milieu, old-fashioned and magnificent at the same time. That is to say, it really introduces nothing new, but offers instead familiar material in hyperbolic form. It represents the optimal realization of a cliché. What was decisive was not so much the details of the plot as the specific interpretation of the roles. With them the story would stand or fall – and both Emil Jannings and Marlene Dietrich fit their roles perfectly. They were capable of summoning the courage needed for the film's doom-laden stylization. Both roles also demanded a special measure of maturity – the seductress, too, had to be worldly wise in order to unleash the catastrophe in a believable way. It was here that Marlene Dietrich's »lost years« came wonderfully to her aid. She was still new, but no longer unexperienced.

Strategically, *The Blue Angel* was a masterpiece of the Berlin film industry, which had planned and supervised its production in an exemplary fashion. Josef von Sternberg evidently also wove himself into the fabric of this well-calculated enterprise, though in this case the high demands he generally made for his contributions were somewhat more modest than usual. In comparison with the other films he had made in Hollywood, both before and later, *The Blue Angel* seems both direct and forthright. The slightly impressionistic flair of his American films is almost completely missing from the German work, and the same can be said for his customary way of distancing himself from the material. All those engaged in this project were agreed that their mission was to erect a monument and that too much individualism might easily endanger it. What was at stake was one of the first German »talkies,« and its commercial success was a matter of great moment. At the same time, the Berlin UFA was backing the return of Emil Jan-

In »The Blue Angel«, 1930
Photo: Mario von Bukovich

nings, who wanted to work in German film studios again after four years in Hollywood. Very important risks were being taken.

Several contestants had been proposed for the female lead, women whose looks were well known and whose movements and gestures had passed the test in other films. Despite the fact that she was hardly the favorite, one dimension of Marlene Dietrich's talents spoke for her even though it had helped her up to now only on the theater stage: her voice. Or to be more precise, her very particular way of singing. It was something that obviously had had to await the advent of the sound film in order to liberate her from her place in the waiting line, where she had been, as often as not, an unemployed silent-screen actress. The sauntering and leisurely manner of her performance, the way in which she could almost sing with her legs, were just what was needed at a time when the quality of the voice was less important than its ability to blend with, to become a part of the body itself. And

In »Destry Rides Again«, 1939
Photo: Ed Estabrook

this is exactly what she had to give to the role. Josef von Sternberg consistently filmed his star with bare arms and legs whenever it was time for her to perform one of her famous songs. Body and voice became one and the same, assisted by the walk, the posture, and the singing style. Her pose sitting on a barrel became almost *the* Marlene Dietrich insignia. The music and texts by the composer Friedrich Holländer corresponded perfectly to the image as created and constituted one more success of the laboratory which had now given birth to a new product. The product was pretty, lively, and dependable, but also rather loud and still quite superficial. The human being beneath had perhaps been given short shrift.

Success is a question of marketability, and the latter's demands are satisfied only by a generous dose of the common touch. A pinch of the spice of vulgarity (in the true meaning of that word) is essential; no one has ever become a star without it. Traces of the ordinary are the necessary accompaniment to whatever else may be art, artifice, and artificiality, and they add, in concentrated form, the human dimension. If the outer appearance does not already possess this attribute (and it generally does), then the role must dictate it. Greta Garbo, for example, was condemned to the stereotype of the sinful woman so that she could climb down from the pedestal of her beauty and return to earth. The »divine« Garbo became a star only when it had been made clear that she was someone who could be touched. Something on the same order happened to Marlene Dietrich after she continued her collaboration with Josef von Sternberg in Hollywood. Her increasingly artificial looks rendered her eventually so remote from common life that palpable blows of fate had to be concocted to compensate for that. Almost without exception she played women of dubious reputation. But earlier, at the time of her breakthrough, it was not only the role itself that was ordinary, but also its physical presentation. This »cheapness« surely contributed to the success.

In the *Blue Angel* stills made by photographer Mario von Bukovich, we see a woman posing who has little time for the niceties of polite society. »Where is the man?« goes one of the songs that Marlene Dietrich sang in those years. The only attribute which we could possibly still consider ladylike is the large hat, and even it seems rather incongruous here. In Hollywood, this kind of packaging gave way to the elegant wardrobe, but it was again called upon when film stars' careers in general threatened to wane in consequence of a kind of aesthetic over-inflation. The price of stars was drastically lowered and the coin of the realm was minted a bit more cheaply. The most obvious indication of that was the turn to adventure movies and Westerns; by the very nature of such entertainments, rougher customs were now in the saddle, and there was a great demand for chummy, heart-of-gold types. Appropriate to the new style were the old tight corsets, bodices, and close-fitting jerseys. The 1939 film *Destry Rides Again* was successful in ushering in the intimate bar room ambiance once again, and it thrived well into the fifties. No matter if Marlene Dietrich was in the Wild West, the South Seas, or in post-war Berlin, she was always the center of attention in a world ruled by men who were anything but gentlemen. It was not until nearly the end of her public career

– and in her stage appearances, above all – that she again moved in the elegant atmosphere of nightclub, varieté, and international hotel. And even here some of the old »rough« songs remained; the tinny clatter of the »Berlin Sound« still had its place.

HOLLYWOOD

With *The Blue Angel,* the German star Marlene Dietrich had been born. Her transsubstantiation into a universally recognized myth was to be the next step, and that, of course, could happen only in the one place on earth that was properly equipped: Hollywood. Only here could the technical facilities be found which, guided by its superior know-how, were capable of the complex procedure known as the styling of a star. The American film industry was incomparable in its efficiency; Europe could not possibly keep up with it. On her way to Hollywood, however, Marlene Dietrich made a stopover which has received attention only recently. After landing in the USA and before her journey to California, the photographer Irving Chidnoff in New York took a number of pictures that reveal her metamorphosis from a European »beauty« to an American film actress. They had been commissioned by Paramount and aroused the anger and jealousy of Josef von Sternberg, who intended to keep for himself the further development and distribution of his new product – indeed, there had been a contractual agreement to that effect. Chidnoff's photographs were not at all to his liking. Nevertheless, the transition from the earlier style – a kind of borrowing from the art-historical context – to the modern expressiveness of the black-and-white photo which can be seen in these pictures is very revealing: the Raphaelesque elf with her still gentle gaze becomes, in this series, one of the Fates, an intimate of destiny and a herald of passion.

Even though this transformation was necessary, it was fortunately not permitted to go so far as to disavow all connection with the Old World. Josef von Sternberg did not hesitate for an instant in letting the new American star appear as someone with an obviously German background. This was most evident in the film *Blonde Venus* (1932), in which Marlene Dietrich was given the role of an efficient Teutonic hausfrau who lives in the States. Of course, in the unfolding plot she totally transcends the confines of her straitened circumstances and becomes a great theater star – just one of the details in a plot which obviously borrowed much from its star's own biography, including the role of the patron and occasional lover in which Josef von Sternberg doubtless saw himself.

In *Morocco* (1930), her first American film, Marlene Dietrich appeared as a French cabaret singer – first in bow tie and tails, then in a jersey with bare legs – recalling the Berlin milieu of *The Blue Angel* once again. Also the dry, somewhat sluggish interpretation of the plot seemed »German,« and the fatalistic details of the plot had the same effect. The country which gave the film its title supplied a somewhat gloomy background for the whole. Then, in 1931, Marlene Dietrich played an Austrian spy in *Dishonored,* a woman whom love makes a traitor. The scene is laid primarily in Russia, and Marlene Dietrich adapted herself to her surroundings by disguising herself as a peasant girl. The best use of an exotic milieu, however, was in *Shanghai Express* (1932), where she played the heroine of a romantic adventure whose roving expeditions take place along the Shanghai-Peking route. The national origins of the swank leading lady are not revealed, but the unmistakably German name Magdalena gives the secret away.

In *The Scarlet Empress* (1934), Marlene Dietrich was the young Princess Sophie Friederike von Anhalt-Zerbst, who is married to the Czarevitch and must learn to make her own way in a foreign clime. The Russian court, to be sure, reveals strangely threatening aspects, and in fact seems more like a Nordic phantasmagoria. Finally, the story line of *The Devil Is a Woman* (1935) unfolds in an almost bizarre setting, a peculiarly artificial Spain. This was the last film that Marlene Dietrich made with Josef von Sternberg, and the weakest as well. The role of a temperamental Iberian was remote from her talents, and she makes an overblown and hectic impression in it.

The underlying element in all these films derived from the puzzling contradictions among obviously disparate features. The celestially beautiful heroine seems all innocence, although it is made quite clear that just the opposite is true. It was certainly

On the set of »Morocco«, 1930
Photo: Don English

On the set of »Shanghai Express«, 1932
Photo: Don English

not her lethargic behavior that kept the plots going, but the eccentrically exotic settings instead that provided all the surprises. The star was static, white as marble, and fixated only on erotic emotion. All other shades and overtones were furnished by accessories: costumes, decor, and the individual traits of her partners. The goddess who remained immaculate despite all injury strode unaffected through the pandemonium of a synthetic world, whose only possible justification for existence was to enhance her image. The apotheosis as well as the limitation of her stardom had been achieved here; the outlines of a sudden reversal into a kind of narcissistic self-destruction were beginning to be revealed behind the now perfected façade. The sensuous process threatened to turn into a mechanical one.

The principal, if superficial, result of this risky development, however, was that the Marlene Dietrich phenomenon became at this period a unique feast for the eyes. This is true both for the evanescent flow of the moving picture as well as for the still shots, the concentrates of these scenes. What we see is the transformation of a woman to higher and higher stages of beauty, the constant re-creation of an ever-beguiling face. Over the course of the first six years, more than five hundred studio portraits were made of film star P-1167 (Marlene Dietrich's official number at Paramount), a total which was substantially increased after the War, when she returned to her old company. The artistic quality of these photographs is without exception first-class: the lighting, focus, and composition meet the highest professional standards.

Today it is difficult to establish what part the studio photographers played in this and what part was due to Josef von Sternberg himself. The influence of the director must have been substantial – he was famous for the concern he lavished on every detail of his films. In addition, the awaken-

Photo: Anton Bruehl, 1937

ing of a new star was a matter of passionate involvement for him. A great deal of speculation has been wasted on the intricacies of this story, and it is undoubtedly true that he possessed a considerable amount of manic obsessiveness. The love-hate dilemma of the director and his product could perhaps have been resolved if he had been successful in literally transforming the living being into a puppet – or even better, into a robot. The object of his peculiar affection tried as hard as was humanly possible to be a tool of his will, but the final metamorphosis failed as a result of her natural resistance. The tension between them reached the point where he actually endangered her life. The episode which Josef von Sternberg recounts about the air rifle he fired on the set to burst some balloons which were covering her face is distressing enough, but to incorporate this inspiration as part of a carnival scene oversteps the limits of normal human ties.

In the artificial line of the eyebrows, which was now to alter Marlene Dietrich's face in a singular way, there can be detected something of that artistic hypertropia which wants to eradicate the natural in favor of its own »improvements.« The result of this new development was beautiful and at the same time painful – and consequently stimulating in a curious way. But back to the individual pictures which reflect these passions of hers in sublimated form. The course of this genesis had numerous station stops. The first Hollywood photographs still remind us of the poses struck in Berlin; costuming, posture, and glance are in part nearly identical – there is no denying that the German soul incarnate sticks out everywhere. On the other hand, the pictures that show Marlene Dietrich again in tails and topper have an instant fascination. The attributes are still the same as in Berlin, but within half a year a transformation has taken place. The wearer of these clothes has gained substantially more self-assurance and now leans intently toward the observer. The photograph of Marlene Dietrich with the lighting man who is training a spotlight on her is a representation of the »life of a star« *per se*. The creation of this new phenomenon is clearly now accomplished, and the way is open to manipulate it not merely by fixing its image but by letting it reflect itself. Here we have a photograph about the photographing of a beautiful object.

Two years later during the filming of *Shanghai Express,* this formula was repeated in a similar fashion, with Marlene Dietrich sitting before a large mirror which the photographer captures in the photograph we see him making. The positioning of the body and the look on her face reveal much of the certainty that the »motif« has gained in the intervening years. The pose makes a casual, self-aware impression, and the little scene contains a good deal of ambiguity.

Most of the early pictures taken at the Paramount Studios were done by Eugene Robert Richee. He emphasized the romantic side of the personality and still saw it as essentially that of a young girl. The gaze is frequently directed upward in all innocence, even a little rapturously. Gesture and pose dominate in these pictures, but the quality of the subject matter itself is inadequately developed; they do not make a very sensual impression. That was all changed when Don English came on the

In »Shanghai Express«, 1932
Photo: Don English

In »The Devil is a Woman«, 1935
Photo: Paramount

scene. This photographer concentrated on the face and discovered it to be sculpture. The modelling of the head by means of clever lighting was first introduced by him. Mostly, the light falls from above; it accentuates the curve of the brow, the cheekbones, and the chin — and it casts the eyelids in shadow. This latter technique, above all, is important, for it gives the gaze a much greater intensity. The effect of the hair is one of particular silkiness and the diffused consistency imparted to it by the lighting enhances the formal precision of the facial features. In general, the counterplay between the impressionistically shimmering background and the radiantly luminous head is the most essential factor in this photographer's approach. The sculptural quality has become more clearly three-dimensional; its ivory-like solidity appears totally without blemish. What arose here was a kind of new criterion: a beautiful face so absolutely regular that we can scarcely imagine any further improvement.

In the now legendary railroad epic, *Shanghai Express,* all of this reached its utmost visual expression. Of all the Sternberg-Dietrich films this is probably the most classic, both in the harmonic unity of its style and in the succinctness of its subject matter and plot. Wreathed in Travis Banton's creations and photographed by the excellent cameraman Lee Garmes, Marlene Dietrich glides through a luxurious hotel on wheels designed by Hans Drier, the art director for all her Paramount pictures. The ideal image seems to have been achieved here; the model has ascended her pedestal and has been transformed into a work of art.

This modern Galatea experienced the opposite fate of her ancient prototype: here love created the artificial object, not the living human being. In her fifth American film, in fact, Marlene Dietrich acted in a closely related Pygmalion story. In *Song of Songs,* directed by Rouben Mamoulian in 1933, she is a country girl who becomes the lover of a sculptor in the big city. But the nude, pillarlike figure that he carves is eventually destroyed — and the spell is broken.

Photo: George Hoyningen-Huene, 1937

Photo: Edward Steichen, ca. 1936

Josef von Sternberg, who was to make two more films with Marlene Dietrich, evidently did not understand this warning; indeed, he even tried to increase the stylization of his creation. The ultimate point was reached in 1935 with *The Devil Is a Woman*, in which the human being is turned into something like a fetish. Bizarre garments were draped over body and face like the coverings on an exotic goddess, and her gestures and body movements give an over-studied, very mechanical impression. The most artificial human imaginable was thereby created – or to put it more accurately, we now have a work of art made to react like a living creature. But the completion of this unparalleled apotheosis also marks the moment of the crash. The public had almost no comprehension of such a display and stayed away.

THE INTERNATIONAL STYLE

During the period before the marble began to show its cracks, however, a new moment of classicism had arisen. Between 1932 and 1934 photographs of Marlene Dietrich were made, which more than any others form our image of her. Above all, they were the pictures made during the filming of *Shanghai Express, Blonde Venus,* and *The Scarlet Empress.* The photographer Don English followed Josef von Sternberg's intentions so closely that we are tempted to believe they were one and the same person. It is difficult to overlook the fact that his portrait shots were directly influenced by the film close-ups – they have the identical flair and a very similar sensual fluidity about them. Beneath the surface of this calculated aesthetic an erotic current is hidden, one whose decorum is simultaneously touching and perplexing. We find ourselves confronted by the mystery that blossoms behind the façade of something we had supposed was plain and unequivocal. Where is the dividing line between reality and vision?

The art of film unquestionably achieved a high point here. It coincided with a similar development in architecture, design, and fashion. Around 1930, the existence of a movement known as the »International Style« was clearly in evidence, a style of high precision, rationality, and, for all of that, sensuous effects. Exemplary buildings, functional furniture, and beautiful household objects and appliances demonstrated these qualities, as did the simple and concentrated design of posters, the expressive elegance of automobiles, and the pure refinement in fashion design. The Modernism of the twenties, after a phase of experimentation and ferment, had reached with the »International Style« a point of maturity and was creating products that possessed a perennial validity. This applies mostly to the developments in Europe; but soon its influence spread to America. The downfall of the movement in the years following 1933 – when Germany, until then the driving force behind it, was taken over by the National Socialists and obliged to withdraw – led the United States to assume the inheritance and continue its development. The severe and at the same time voluptuous shimmer of Josef von Sternberg's films demonstrated a great affinity with this movement – but at the same time, these films also revealed the risk inherent in this style of becoming too hermetic and remote. This outspoken aesthetic possessed immensely narcissistic traits.

The look of Marlene Dietrich during this period can be seen as the living embodiment of this universal style, whose polyglot image she herself did much to create – and from which she also drew many a detail to enhance her own image. It provided her with both a supportive foil and backdrop and prevented her from seeming too esoteric or isolated. This assistance was absolutely essential, for the avant garde of the day was confined to a relatively limited arena and was dependent on inner solidarity. As always seems to be the case, the validity of what was created at that time only became evident well after the fact of its creation. The »eternal return« factor which Marlene Dietrich enjoys with her public is very like the continuing demand today for objects designed in that period – the tubular steel furniture, for example, which has gone on being produced without change since 1930. Or it is like the admiration for the buildings of Mies van der Rohe, Le Corbusier, and Alvar Aalto which were erected in the thirties. A nearly identical self-awareness, elegance, and internationalism is inherent in all these testimonials to an epoch in the history of style whose exacting demands are still with us today.

Photo: Cecil Beaton, ca. 1935

THE ART OF THE ARTIFICIAL

It can be said that from this period on Marlene Dietrich always remained true to its precepts. Those were the years that gave her image its final form and endowed her with the unique personal style that distinguishes her from all others. From that time on, the manner of dressing which she favored consisted always of variations on the fashions she had adopted in the thirties. It was also the time when she acquired her intimidating knowledge of lighting and photographic techniques. However, the self-assurance which she had developed by that period was something that others were not always able to muster on her behalf. The lapidary fact of her beauty clearly prompted others to try to contradict it and to shroud it by synthetic means that exceeded any acceptable norm. Perfection can evidently be an irritant and is something that can be endured by its admirers only at certain times. The manneristic experiments which Josef von Sternberg undertook in his last two films with Marlene Dietrich can perhaps be seen in this light. The same is true of many of the pictures of her taken by famous photographers of the day in private sessions. One can sense in them a strange sort of personal ambitiousness in their insistence on overloading the image with costuming and window-dressing as a foil to the human being in their

Photo: Horst P. Horst, 1942

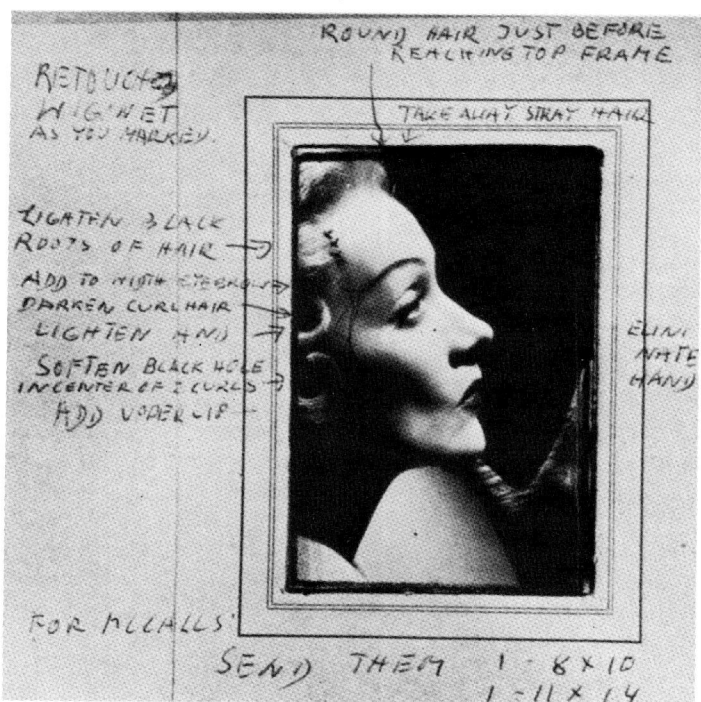

Photo: John Engstead, ca. 1950
With Marlene Dietrich's instructions on how to retouch the photo (see plate 110)

midst. As a result, the face becomes little more than a set-piece in a sea of props.

To be specific, these are the photographs by Cecil Beaton, Edward Steichen, and George Hoyningen-Huene taken in the mid-thirties. They were made for reasons and under conditions altogether different from anything hitherto. It was no longer a matter of capturing specific scenes or poses from her films; instead, sessions completely removed from the atmosphere of the film studio were arranged, one-time events complete in themselves. What formerly was done as a series of still shots now had to be done in a concentrated way – it was a matter of capturing a few highly stylized moments. Both the tradition of classic portrait photography and the techniques of theater practice played a part in this procedure. Backdrops and props had important roles, to which was then added the artificial drama of spotlights. The poses could be exaggerated, and affectation as a stylistic device was allowed to permeate the whole. Something that would have quickly been unmasked in the ultimately down-to-earth world of the film studio could assert itself here and was justified by the artistic brilliance of the end result.

The extraordinary efforts which Beaton and Steichen made were surely due in part to the demands put upon them by their star subject. It was considered a great honor to be permitted to photograph Marlene Dietrich. On the other hand, the photographers' ambition insisted on its own satisfaction; for these men likewise enjoyed a reputation as stars. And so it was natural that the twin facets of this synthetic art-form mutually enhanced and intensified each other and led to a kind of apotheosis. All the same, we can also detect a certain playfulness on the part of the participants, a gentle irony which lets us see that the seriousness of the whole enterprise was not permitted to be overdone. The »window-dressing«, for example, can now and then be detected as being pretty cheap stuff: plaster of Paris, gauze, and netting – and those hats are really nothing one would ever wear.

The perfection and artificial bravura of these photographic images can occasionally make us forget that to a great extent they are intended as ends in themselves. Their detached and noncommittal quality is not revealed until we study them at some length. Where flowers, wallpaper, feathers, and other props are made to seem co-equal with hands, faces, and hair, our sympathy feels itself to have been duped and finally ceases to react to the intended effect. Yet despite it all, the superficial materialism of these photographs probably signifies more than the arrangement of their details reveals at first glance. The accumulation of all these aids and props is yet another attempt to achieve a transposition. The piling up of material objects into often quite disparate agglomerations is aiming at a metamorphosis into the surreal. The photographer Horst P. Horst went the furthest in this direction. He was a clever pupil of the work of Salvador Dali and drew heavily from it. His pictures of Marlene Dietrich, however, reveal a somewhat different approach through the unusually concentrated and intense effect they have on us. If one can compare them with the other work of the artist, one is tempted to speculate that in this case the subject herself was in command. Or perhaps it is merely that Horst P. Horst knew perfectly well whom he had before him.

In any case, the subject being photographed was thoroughly familiar with the effect her pictures made and for that reason was active in stipulating their details. Her careful directions for retouching a proof made by John Engstead provide an excellent example of this. Here ambition is speaking. Professionalism does not overlook a single detail. The lady knew who she was and what she wanted.

Photo: Irving Penn, 1948

THE CIPHERS OF THE PERSONALITY

Suddenly, in the pictures which a number of photographers made of Marlene Dietrich after the war, all artificiality and all magic are gone. It is not only that the person has matured, but the very way of seeing her has taken on more concrete forms. The latent cynicism of the pre-war photos is dismissed, and an uncommon, almost puritanical, seriousness dominates the scene. Irving Penn and Milton H. Greene succeeded at the time in producing images which (instead of the customary props) made use of a new code language. By this period, the entire world had gotten to know the famous subject – and thus it became possible to restrict the image to its essentials: the face, natu-

Photo: Milton H. Greene, 1952

rally, but astonishingly, the hair and legs alone are sufficient. It amounts to an unprecedented case of popularity based on universally recognizable and unique characteristics. It is this that now, finally, enters the lens undisguised and candidly and communicates with us by means of gesture and pose alone.

It was possible to bring this reversal about at a time when Marlene Dietrich was playing only sporadically in films. We are no longer confronted by someone who is just a serial duplicate of her diverse roles but by the very source and owner of these roles herself. The impressive artificiality of her life up to now begins to give way to the high art of unmediated expression.

The photograph by Milton H. Greene was perhaps not originally intended in this sense, but when it was suddenly there, it proved to have captured certain completely unmistakable features. It is not so much the curves of the celebrated legs that carry the message here, as it is the way they are arranged. There is courage in them, and an outspoken indifference to whatever might befall their owner. We see here the physical expression of someone whose independence must be acknowledged as much as her honesty.

Irving Penn placed Marlene Dietrich in front of the brightly lit backdrop familiar from so much of his other work. But whereas his subjects generally seem too arranged, their personalities over-exposed, that effect is not present here. This subject was not putty in his hands. The intense look on her face seems to be asking if the moment about to be recorded is concentrated enough. The woman who is portrayed here is clearly an active participant in the genesis of the picture – and we are witnesses to a very intricate situation. The slightly skeptical way in which she holds her body only adds to our impression of having been brouht in on a dialogue where only the truth counts. The bright, unflattering light on the somewhat dour features enhances the same effect; it not only illuminates the very center of the picture but in one stroke lays bare the whole content of the scene. The great dark shape of her back, finally, functions as a unique entry into the very essence of the image.

Here, too, the decisiveness with which the subject comports herself is overwhelming; her tenacity and determination evoke our admiration. It was risky enough that she allowed herself to be photographed in this pose; on top of that, the technical approach itself is diametrically opposed to the earlier practice of soft transitions and the incorporation of sensuous details. It is, in fact, an affront to that well-established style. But in its place, we now have elements that impart a clear picture of the personality itself. Instead of a transfiguration, the kernel of the myth is revealed. At the same time, there was ushered in a new photographic style whose revelatory impact could henceforth be neither denied nor forgotten. To be sure, it was never again applied quite so consistently as it was here; yet it is a fact that all subsequent photographs of Marlene Dietrich have a similarly forthright and deliberate quality.

ENDURANCE

The films she made during this period are not nearly so powerful; the new possibilities opened by these portraits barely influenced them. Nevertheless, a few attempts were made to render her roles less superficial, a bit deeper; darker shadows were now permitted. In *A Foreign Affair* (1948) Marlene Dietrich plays the former lover of a highly placed Nazi who attempts to survive in postwar Berlin. In its day, this Billy Wilder film was felt to be outspokenly cynical and was sharply criticized for it. Two years later in *Stage Fright*, she is a famous singer who instigates the murder of her husband. Here, however, her gorgeous looks are no longer used as a cover for unrecognized but eventually triumphant innocence, as they once were in her early von Sternberg films; instead, they now conceal the depths of a highly questionable character.

It was not until 1957 that Marlene Dietrich was given a role in which she was able to reveal all the facets of her talent at once. *Witness for the Prosecution* is the story of a German woman who devises a clever ruse to exonerate her British husband, indicted for murder, but who then kills him when she learns that his crime had been committed for a female rival. The courtroom of the Old Bailey provides the backdrop for the action. The ingredients of the plot include elements of tawdry glitter (in a

In »Judgment at Nuremberg«, 1961
Photo: Anon.

flashback the star is seen as cabaret entertainer with accordion) as well as of courage, fidelity, and devotion. In addition, she is imbued with a deep sense of justice which finally forces her to seek revenge; the offense to her pride leads to her own crime. The pathos of the story was much praised at the time. Billy Wilder had chosen the material expressly for Marlene Dietrich; he clearly had a precise feeling for the effect she could achieve with it.

The circle was complete with *Judgment at Nuremberg* in 1961. This ambitious film by Stanley Kramer deals with the condemnation and sentencing of Nazi war criminals, and in it Marlene Dietrich plays the widow of a German general whom the Americans have executed. Her role called for a dry, severe, somewhat statuesque appearance; yet its total effect remains multi-layered: the erotic signals she conveys are undiminished. What we are shown is a German patriot with the international flair of a great seductress, her age and background notwithstanding. Toward the end of the picture, the presiding American judge proposes a relationship, but he is rebuffed. There is one absolutely symmetrical, resolutely black-and-white still which captures the character of the protagonist in a single concentrated image. Its inexorable frontality permits no glossing over, and the sharpness and severity of the lighting reveal the inconsistencies as well as the virtues of the personality.

This somewhat ceremonial photograph epitomizes what the film itself does: it erects a monument to the star. Once again, the dependable product is vigorously promoted. As so often in the past, role, set, and costume fit each other splendidly. The reminder of her Prussian origins is just as deliberately introduced here as the summons to loyalty, discipline, and composure – and all of it is suffused with a sensual feminine appeal. The scope of this last important film appearance was not great, but given the size of the role, every calculation proved once again to be the right one. Marlene Dietrich left the screen as a star whose reputation was fully intact.

These last films emphasize the heroic traits of the actress and almost completely eliminate the nonchalant and sentimental ones. It was at this point in her career that the role of film tragedienne was complemented by that of the entertainer in a series of unforgettable stage appearances. It was here that her earlier talents again came to the fore: heart, brashness, and the allure of her extravagant showmanship. They were all calculated to assure the audience that the whole performance was nothing more than a trick and to make sure that her part in it maintained proper proportion. Aristocratic, rich, and totally sure of herself, the honky-tonk singer of *The Blue Angel* returned and reported on all her successes since those days. Luxury had long since replaced the cheap glitter. The triumph was complete.

Whereas in 1930 her voice was only one of the factors in her breakthrough, now, twenty-five years later, it was the essential element in her second career. It became the vehicle for the more complex, richer, and more spiritual aspects of her personality which now predominated over the purely physical attributes – but these, too, continued to be carefully nurtured and exhibited. The splendor of her appearance was undiminished. The first half of the show was performed in white tie, topper, and tails, a reminiscence of earlier days; and it was beautiful, touching, and a glorious aid to audience recall. The second act, however, was always done in elegant, shimmering gowns, skin-tight, slinky, and clinging; she became an exclamation mark, the incarnation of seductiveness under careful control. Her costume made headlines, not because it was particularly original, but because the figure and its covering seemed to have achieved total fusion. The sequins seemed to be an integral part of the body itself. After the androgynous apparition of a woman in men's apparel, here was a mermaid in glistening scales. And to complete the effect, a white and foaming wave of fur flowed over the enchantress. The ambivalence of this sequence might seem perplexing at first encounter, but it soon became clear how the double aspect harmonized. In all of it the star remained beyond reach; its enticement was there, but so was the illusion. The photographs of these stage appearances show once more the essence of her art in the beauty of its perfection.

THE METAMORPHOSIS

Is there still a modicum of the human being in it? Or has the person in the intervening years fused completely with the creation that has been produced in her image? I believe the latter is the case. Although my conjecture is naturally open to contradiction, and although it runs counter to the illusory belief concerning the nature of illusion, I still think it is valid. Fifty years of artificial existence, endured by dint of self-discipline, must have created someone whose individual traits have merged with and finally been subsumed by the official image which she has given to the world. The power of metamorphosis cannot be reversed, especially not when such a mutation has been determined from the start and then pursued as the whole point of one's life. It represents fulfillment and produces the one true happiness: ever-present reality as opposed to remembered reality. Illusion is thereby reduced to no more than the faith that some few fragments of childhood can be preserved.

Seen from this perspective, this hypothesis can be a confirmation of one's own standpoint, which is always identical to that of the spectator who is able to see only the artificial image. And it is broad-based, for it can claim to be universally understood. It is popular judgment based on popular perception. Who is there who can really say that he knows Marlene Dietrich? Yet there are untold numbers of people who have identical images of her. That is what counts.

Is it possible that the star herself might agree with this account? In a long interview which the actor and director Maximilian Schell conducted with Marlene Dietrich not long ago, she rejected all questions about her personal life and persisted in turning the topic of conversation to her life in films. For her (though she admitted it only in passing) this is the essence of everything she has done.

And is this not truly admirable? Without evasiveness, without sentimentality, she testified here to a life of fulfillment that for most others would be only a dream or a hope, something that is almost never realized. And yet, her personality has not become some minor adjunct to her second life; instead they have fused, become one and the same. The result has been a unique existence for her, an existence that retains all its human dimension. But it is no longer free and arbitrary. Chance and accident have become things foreign to her. In exchange for this redemption from earthly vicissitudes, however, her transformation into a human being as a form of art has been a small price to pay. Presumably the one is impossible without the other.

Klaus-Jürgen Sembach

THE PLATES

The film titles in the captions of the following plates are intended to indicate the approximate dates of the photographs which are not necessarily stills from those films.

Berlin, ca. 1926   Photo: W. von Gudenberg

Vienna, 1927   Photo: d'Ora

Vienna, 1927 Photo: d'Ora

Berlin, ca. 1929   Photo: Ufa

»Die Frau, nach der man sich sehnt« (»Three Loves«), Berlin, 1929   Photo: Terra

»Der blaue Engel«, Berlin, 1930   Photo: Mario von Bukovich

»Der blaue Engel«, Berlin, 1930   Photo: Mario von Bukovich

Berlin, 1929 Photo: Alfred Eisenstaedt

New York, 1930   Photo: Irving Chidnoff

New York, 1930 Photo: Irving Chidnoff

New York, 1930   Photo: Irving Chidnoff

1930 Photo: Eugene Robert Richee

1930   Photo: Eugene Robert Richee

»Morocco«, 1930   Photo: Eugene Robert Richee

»Morocco«, 1930   Photo: Eugene Robert Richee

»Morocco«, 1930   Photo: Eugene Robert Richee

»Morocco«, 1930   Photo: Eugene Robert Richee

»Morocco«, 1930   Photo: Eugene Robert Richee

»Morocco«, 1930   Photo: Eugene Robert Richee

»Morocco«, 1930   Photo: Eugene Robert Richee

»Dishonored«, 1931   Photo: Eugene Robert Richee

»Dishonored«, 1931   Photo: Eugene Robert Richee

»Dishonored«, 1931   Photo: Eugene Robert Richee

»Morocco«, 1930   Photo: Eugene Robert Richee

»Morocco«, 1930   Photo: Eugene Robert Richee

»Morocco«, 1930   Photo: Don English

»Shanghai Express«, 1932   Photo: Eugene Robert Richee

»Shanghai Express«, 1932   Photo: Eugene Robert Richee

»Shanghai Express«, 1932 Photo: Eugene Robert Richee

»Shanghai Express«, 1932   Photo: Eugene Robert Richee

»Shanghai Express«, 1932   Photo: Don English

»Shanghai Express«, 1932   Photo: Don English

»Shanghai Express«, 1932   Photo: Don English

»Shanghai Express«, 1932   Photo: Don English

»Shanghai Express«, 1932   Photo: Don English

»Shanghai Express«, 1932   Photo: Don English

»Shanghai Express«, 1932   Photo: Don English

»Shanghai Express«, 1932   Photo: Don English

»Shanghai Express«, 1932 Photo: Don English

Hollywood, 1932 Photo: Anon.

»Shanghai Express«, 1932   Photo: Don English

»Shanghai Express«, 1932   Photo: Don English

»Shanghai Express«, 1932   Photo: Don English

»Shanghai Express«, 1932   Photo: Don English

»Blonde Venus«, 1932   Photo: Eugene Robert Richee

»Blonde Venus«, 1932   Photo: Eugene Robert Richee

»Blonde Venus«, 1932   Photo: Don English

Ca. 1933 Photo: Eugene Robert Richee

Ca. 1933 Photo: Eugene Robert Richee

Ca. 1933 Photo: Eugene Robert Richee

»Song of Songs«, 1933   Photo: Eugene Robert Richee

1934   Photo: William Walling

1934   Photo: William Walling

1934   Photo: William Walling

1934 Photo: William Walling

1934   Photo: William Walling

Ca. 1934   Photo: Eugene Robert Richee

»Scarlet Empress«, 1934   Photo: Don English

1934   Photo: William Walling

1934   Photo: William Walling

1934   Photo: William Walling

1934   Photo: William Walling

1934 Photo: William Walling

»Desire«, 1936   Photo: Eugene Robert Richee

1936   Photo: Anton Bruehl

1935   Photo: Eugene Robert Richee

1935   Photo: Eugene Robert Richee

1935   Photo: Eugene Robert Richee

1935   Photo: Eugene Robert Richee

1935 Photo: Eugene Robert Richee

1935 Photo: Eugene Robert Richee

»The Devil is a Woman«, 1935   Photo: Eugene Robert Richee

»The Devil is a Woman«, 1935   Photo: Eugene Robert Richee

Ca. 1936   Photo: Edward Steichen

Ca. 1935 Photo: Cecil Beaton

Ca. 1935 Photo: Cecil Beaton

Ca. 1937 Photo: Cecil Beaton

»Angel«, 1937   Photo: George Hoyningen-Huene

»Angel«, 1937   Photo: Eugene Robert Richee

»Garden of Allah«, 1936   Photo: Kenneth Alexander

»Knight Without Armor«, 1937   Photo: Turnbridge

1937 Photo: Don English

83

»Angel«, 1937   Photo: Don English

»Angel«, 1937   Photo: Don English

»Angel«, 1937   Photo: Don English

Ca. 1937   Photo: George Hurrell

Ca. 1937 Photo: George Hurrell

»Destry Rides Again«, 1939   Photo: Ed Estabrook

»Destry Rides Again«, 1939   Photo: Ray Jones

»Seven Sinners«, 1940 Photo: John Engstead

Ca. 1940 Photo: Nikolas Muray

1940   Photo: Ray Jones

»Manpower«, 1941   Photo: Scotty Welbourne

»Manpower«, 1941   Photo: Scotty Welbourne

1940 Photo: Scotty Welbourne

1940 Photo: Scotty Welbourne

1942   Photo: Laszlo Willinger

1942   Photo: Laszlo Willinger

1942 Photo: Horst P. Horst

1942 Photo: Horst P. Horst

1942 Photo: Horst P. Horst

»Martin Roumagnac«, 1946   Photo: Anon.

1947   Photo: A. L. »Whitey« Schaefer

»Stage Fright«, 1950   Photo: Warner Brothers

»No Highway«, 1951   Photo: Ted Reed

»Stage Fright«, 1950   Photo: Davis Boulton

Ca. 1950 Photo: Erwin Blumenfeld

Ca. 1950　Photo: Horst P. Horst

Ca. 1950   Photo: John Engstead

110

1948 Photo: Irving Penn

1952   Photo: Milton H. Greene

1952 Photo: Milton H. Greene

M. D., Turban by Dior, The Ritz, 1955 Paris   Photo: Richard Avedon

Ca. 1955 Photo: Lord Snowdon

Cafe de Paris, London, 1955 Photo: Norman Parkinson

Ca. 1955   Photo: John Engstead

Bad Kissingen, 1960   Photo: Harald Meisert

Théâtre de l'Étoile, Paris 1959   Photo: François Gragnon

»Judgment at Nuremberg«, 1961   Photo: United Artists

1960 Photo: Liselotte Strelow

Berlin, 1960   Photo: Harry Croner

Munich, 1960 Photo: Herbert List

JOSEF VON STERNBERG: THE MAKING OF MARLENE

When extreme sentiments blend in the deep of a person, when they burst out, and when the entire mind flows like lava from a volcano – the cold calculations of reason have not presided over this emission, and who knows when and where the work was started?   Paul Gauguin

Marlene Dietrich is no ordinary woman; her ability to enrapture our jury of peers is remarkable. In Israel she was cheered when she sang in the German language, taboo on the stage until then. But whether there or in Argentina, in Las Vegas, in Wiesbaden, in Paris, or wherever it may be, she waves the banner of her indebtedness, includes me in her act, and, since few are familiar with even the most rudimentary functioning of a film director, has almost succeeded in making me a subsidiary requisite. Her constant praise is rated as one of her admirable virtues – by others, not by me. She has never ceased to proclaim that I taught her everything. Among the many things I did not teach her was to be garrulous about me.

A ship now sails the seas, registered as the *Marlene;* numberless children grow up with a name unknown to the world not long ago. »Marlene« is a contraction of »Maria Magdalene«, two names not often found in one person. Before becoming reconciled to being known as Marlene Dietrich, she pleaded with me to change her name, as no non-German could pronounce it correctly. The plea was ignored and she was told, correctly pronounced or not, the name would become quite well known. She attached no value to it when I met her, nor did she attach value to anything else so far as I could ascertain, with the exception of her baby daughter, a musical saw, and some recordings by a singer called Whispering Jack Smith. She was inclined to jeer at herself and at others, though she was extremely loyal to friends (many of whom were not always loyal to her) and quick to feel pity and to help those who flattered her for qualities that were not always flattering. She was frank and outspoken to a degree that some might have termed tactless. Her personality was one of extreme sophistication and of an almost childish simplicity.

As I came to know more about her I also became familiar with the conditions that had produced her, her family, and the circle around her. Her energy to survive and to rise above her environment must have been fantastic. She was subject to severe depressions, though these were balanced by periods of unbelievable vigor. To exhaust her was not possible; it was she who exhausted others, and with enthusiasms few were able to share. At times provoking because of her peculiar superstitions, she balanced this with uncommon good sense which approached scholarship. The theatre was in her blood, and she was familiar with every parasite in it. Her reading consisted of Hamsun, Lagerlöf, Hofmannsthal and Hölderlin. She worshiped Rilke and knew by heart the writings of Erich Kästner. She gave me a book of the last-mentioned poet in which she strongly underlined one particular poem. Were it in English, the sense of it would be this:

Gloom comes and goes without a cause
And one is full of only emptiness.
One isn't sick, nor is one well.
It is as if the soul were indisposed.

One wants to be alone, but then again with others
One's disposition may be out of joint.
The stars appear to be mere freckles.
One isn't sick, one only suffers.

One wants to run, but finds no place to hide.
It is as if retreat led to the grave.
The distant glance shows but dark spots.
One likes to die – or take a fortnight's leave.*

---

*This is a free translation of three verses from a seven-verse poem entitled »Traurigkeit, die jeder kennt« from *Doktor Erich Kästners Lyrische Hausapotheke* (Vienna, Mähr.-Ostrau, Atrium-Verlag A. G. Basel, 1936).

Despite her melancholy, she was well dressed and believed herself to be beautiful, though until this was radically altered by me she had been photographed to look like a female impersonator. There are many unflattering photographs of her pre-*Blue Angel* period in existence, portraying an inhibited subject almost anxious to hide. Nevertheless she distributed them to all and sundry with the air of bestowing a priceless gift. One of them is in my files. Scribbled on it is »Ich bin nichts ohne Dich« (I am nothing without you). This accolade I declined then, and I do so now, though I must accept some of the responsibility for her image in my films. Never before had I met so beautiful a woman who had been so thoroughly discounted and undervalued.

Some of the admirers she subsequently collected came to me to state bitterly that they had sought in vain the image of her that flashed on the screen. Amusingly enough, a famous writer who should have known better went so far as to say that I had done him considerable harm by endowing her with a personality not her own. I did not endow her with a personality that was not her own; one sees what one wants to see, and I gave her nothing that she did not already have. What I did was to dramatize her attributes and make them visible for all to see; though, as there were perhaps too many, I concealed some. There was no reason for anyone to complain, as what most men seek in a woman is not difficult to locate. Had I included *Caveat emptor* in the main title of *The Blue Angel,* no one would have paid heed anyway.

About a hundred years ago the ruins of a monumental temple were found in a steaming Cambodian jungle. Those who had worshiped there must have prayed to the wrong gods, for the race vanished, and what is left of Angkor Vat must crumble too. When I was there huge trees were encircling its remains with their giant roots as if to crush what was left. An army of sculptors had engraved a legend on its wall which shows Vishnu churning a sea of milk with the aid of a legion of demons on one side and with numberless monkeys, led by Hanuman, on the other. The myth that this commotion illustrates has it that the ocean was agitated for a thousand years to bring to its tossing surface a woman who was to charm the world. Not much more than a few weeks were at my disposal for a similar feat, and I had very few to help, though I did have a turbulent ocean.

My ocean was Berlin in the fall of 1929. The war that had ended eleven years before had left the capital of a once proud Germany physically intact. Other things had happened that proved as destructive and more so than if the city had been turned into rubble – something the next war was to accomplish. When I arrived, Berlin had barely recovered from upheavals that its people should have remembered. Following in the wake of the defeat of the German Empire, the fleet had revolted, what was left of the army had scurried to hide, officers had had their epaulettes ripped off by the mobs, and the emperor had fled; all this was a prelude to political confusion, chaos, starvation, and a currency inflation that bordered on insanity. Stamp collectors can leaf through their albums and note that the postage required to mail a letter advanced in less than a year to a sum that staggers the imagination: eighty billion marks. Social currency collapsed as well and morality became a curiosity. Paper money that was worth a fortune the day before would not buy a loaf of bread the following morning. A people once strong and arrogant had been leveled to animals foraging for food. All normal values had become obsolete.

When nothing is left to be lost, reservoirs of previously untapped energies can be released, energies that are not easily controlled. The victors, those who had brought a proud enemy to its knees, had not yet learned that too much must not happen to too many. The years that followed the catastrophe produced not only masses of beggars, swindlers, criminals, whores, dope addicts, and degenerates, not only artists who often thrive when others perish but also demagogues and eager listeners, and finally, as was found out to our sorrow, a vicious dictator, who upset the entire world.

This ocean was seething when I was called to explore it. I lived in a quiet hotel on the river Spree, a rest house in the midst of a maelstrom, and to leave it was like shooting the rapids. At night, when I went out to dine, it was not unusual for something that sat next to me, dressed as a woman, to powder its nose with a large puff that a moment ago had seemed to be a breast. To differentiate between the sexes was, to make an understatement, confusing. Not only did men masquerade as females, wearing false eyelashes, beauty spots, rouge and veil, but the woods were full of females who looked and functioned like men. A third species, defying definition, circulated to lend itself to whatever the occasion offered. To raise an eyebrow at all this branded one as a tourist. To quote Erich Kästner's popular poem, it began with the devastating »In the place where others have a soul, she had a hole.«

Berlin demanded distraction, and those who supplied it demanded their share. Cabarets, theatres, and night clubs teemed with actors and actresses. No companion of theirs was twice the same; they were surcharged and stimulated night and day; they slipped in and out of their haunts like eels. It would be wrong to suppose that all of the city was in hectic pursuit of questionable values, but enough was in sight to give that impression. The public display included girls in boots with whips in hand, waiting to beat up their patrons; and another group, flaunting pigtails and schoolbooks, paraded to appeal to those who hurried to meet them with set jaw and clenched fists. Outwardly Berlin in 1929 was an evocation by Goya, Beardsley, Marquis de Bayros, Zille, Baudelaire, and Huysmans.

The organization that had brought me there was financed by Alfred Hugenberg. A graduate of the old Prussian ministry, a director of Krupp's, as powerful as any man in the Germany of that day, he also financed the rise of Adolf Hitler. I did not meet Hugenberg until three years later when I revisited the city and was invited to dine with him. At dinner he admitted that he had opposed the making of *The Blue Angel,* but that he now was glad that he had been persuaded to permit it, and in an unguarded moment he confided that he had supported Hitler, which he now regretted. It was known that the book on which some of the material of my film was based had been on Hugenberg's black list for years. A previous chapter, dealing with Jannings, relates how this book came to be selected. Evidently it had not been easy for Hugenberg to harmonize his political convictions with the making of money, and he finally lost them both.

In the intervening three years since the filming of *The Blue Angel* the city had not changed, though there was a signal of things to come the morning following the dinner with Hugenberg. The cab that carried me to the airport on February 27, 1933, was delayed in front of the burning Reichstag, and my driver volunteered the information that the Nazis had set fire to the Parliament building so as to be able to whip up sentiment against the Communists. I did not see Berlin again until 1960. It had undergone many changes, some for the better and some for the worse.

The Berlin of 1929 was the background of »the woman who was to charm the world.« Heinrich Mann's book contained a brilliant chart of an amoral woman whose flesh brought about the downfall of a high school professor. My associates had told me that the portrait of the seductive harlot was anchored in the personal history of the author. Be that as it may, one stately and dignified elderly German lady, thought to be the original, had already been presented to me as a prospect for the part of the alluring female. But along with most others that were being lined up for my approval, she could have played Circe only to one blindfolded. And as I proceeded to dictate the scenario, everyone's inamorata was ushered into the office to unveil charms that had they been gathered in one individual might have been more than desirable. One had the necessary eyes, another a graceful posture, one legs that weren't knock-kneed, and still another a voice that promised deviltry, but I could not see how half a dozen different women could be made to play one part.*

All the other members of the cast had been chosen. An able staff was at my beck and call. Missing was Lola, so named by me and inspired by Wedekind's Lulu. In planning the work I had decided on an elephantine cast of supporting players, in order to have its collective bulk reduce the visible fat of my leading man, who was adding to his bulges day by day on the assumption that he had to fortify his body for the strenuous task ahead. Berlin was bursting at the seams with actresses padded with rolling fat, but none seemed to have rolled it where it might have been viewed favorably.

---

*Much later, somewhere in Europe – possibly in Nikita Balieff's Chauve-Souris – I saw this done in an operatic satire which constantly switched performers as their separate talents were needed.

I had a model in mind for the figure needed to balance my conception of Lola, and I rejected one actress after the other for no better reason than that she was different from the one I had visualized. The specifications had been drawn up by Félicien Rops, and though his model had lived in another century and in a different country, a duplicate had to be found in Berlin.

As the deadline for starting the film approached, an uneasiness made itself felt. A rumor began to circulate that the woman I sought was not on earth. In turning over the pages of a trade catalogue that contained a photograph of every actress in Germany I had paused at a flat and uninteresting portrait of a Fräulein Dietrich, and, asking my assistant about her as I had asked about many others, saw him shrug his shoulders while saying, »Der Popo ist nicht schlecht, aber brauchen wir nicht auch ein Gesicht?« (Not at all bad from the rear, but do we not also need a face?) So she was promptly relegated to the others and forgotten until, by accident, I attended a play by Georg Kaiser called *Zwei Krawatten,* in which members* of my cast already chosen were performing.

It was in that play that I saw Fräulein Dietrich in the flesh, if that it can be called, for she had wrapped herself up as if to conceal every part of her body. What little she had to do on that stage was not easily apparent; I remember only one line of dialogue. Here was the face I had sought, and, so far as I could tell, a figure that did justice to it. Moreover, there was something else I had not sought, something that told me that my search was over. She leaned against the wings with a cold disdain for the buffoonery, in sharp contrast to the effervescence of the others, who had been informed that I was to be treated to a sample of the greatness of the German stage. She had heard that I was in the audience, but as she did not consider herself involved, she was indifferent to my presence.

There was an impressive poise about her (not natural, as it turned out, for she was an exuberant bubbler when not restrained) that made me certain that she would lend a classic stature to the turmoil the woman of my film would have to create. Here was not only a model who had been designed by Rops, but Toulouse-Lautrec would have turned a couple of handsprings had he laid eyes on her. Her appearance was ideal; what she did with it was something else again. That would be my concern. The making of a film cannot be compared to any other creative labor. There are too many factors, too many loose ends, each one of which if not properly gathered can wreck the project. My instincts, not always on the alert, had been strong enough this time to hold out until I had found the most important component of the film about to be made. Without the electricity of a new and exciting female, the film would have been no more than an essay reflecting on the stupiditiy of a school tyrant. In the morning I confronted my associates to inquire why the actress who had so effectively graced the proscenium last night had not been proposed for the part. A barrage of protest greeted my complaint: this actress was no actress. I had no wish to discuss the spurious definitions applied to acting, and merely mentioned that the start to become an actress had to be made one time or another. The chorus then chanted that in her case the start had been made not only once but a dozen times. When I insisted that the matter should be gone into more thoroughly, Mr. Jannings suggested that the time thus wasted could be used to better advantage were I to take him out and treat him to a second breakfast, as it always made him desperately hungry to contemplate the problem of other performers in a film designed to star him. It was nine-fifteen in the morning, and I told him to go out and sample every sausage in Berlin at my expense. This permitted him to exit in high humor while I gave instructions to my office that the lady in question should be produced therein as soon as possible.

As Fräulein Dietrich sat in the office late that afternoon she made not the slightest effort to intensify my interest. She was seated in a corner of a sofa facing my desk, her eyes downcast, a study in apathy. Across from me was a bundle of womanhood who was vital to my film, attempting to blot herself out. Clad in a heliotrope winter suit, with hat and gloves to match, and furs, she appeared to have come to visit me in order to take a much-needed rest. To draw her out of her lethargy I inquired why her reputation as an actress seemed to be a doubtful one. For a moment she looked at

---

*Hans Albers and Rosa Valetti.

her gloved hands, and then, as if she had exposed too much, hid them quickly in back of her. This shrouded lady in front of me was not going to make the task of converting her into a tiger an easy one.

As I was trying to fuse her actual image with what was in my mind, Erich Pommer, flanked by a jovial Jannings, entered and with admirable directness asked her to take off her bonnet and walk up and down. This was the usual ceremonial of interviewing an actress to determine at once whether she was bald or had a limp. She complied by strolling through the small room with bovine listlessness, not seeming to look where she was going, and giving me the impression that any moment she might bump into the furniture. Her eyes were completely veiled. The two experts exchanged telling glances and, one clearing his throat while the other delicately scratched his ear, left the room after a couple of limp handshakes that were meant to give me their opinion. Afterward Jannings informed me that a cow veils her eyes only when giving birth to a calf. This was not the only disparaging remark I was to hear, for that night several of my alarmed helpers rushed to the theatre to check my judgment and returned to tell me that they had seen nothing that was worth looking at, and a friendly suggestion was made that I should have my eyesight checked.

Miss Dietrich remained standing after the producer and the star had delivered their unspoken verdict. No doubt she had expected nothing else, but she looked at the door which had closed behind them with a deep look of contempt which she then transferred to me as if I had been responsible for the unnecessary humiliation. I asked her to please be seated again and studied her. Obviously she had a great deal of vitality, though not knowing what to do with it she concealed it completely. I then proceeded to give her a rough idea of what was in store for her, and she became alerted enough to respond in a childish voice that she had been under the impression that she might be wanted for a minor part, not for the leading role. I told her that this was not so, and that she was perfect for what I had in mind. This apparently only made her indignant, as if I had slighted her. She came out of her shell long enough to inform me that she could not act, that it was impossible for anyone to photograph her to look like herself, that she had been treated badly by the press and, to my surprise, she also revealed that she had been featured in three films in which she had not been good. This was a novel experience for me, for no one to whom I had ever offered a part had volunteered to apprise me of failures.

Actually I found out later that she had not only been ineffective in three films but in nine, and had been in musicals, not only in the chorus of hits such as *Broadway* but had been featured by many talented men. Apparently everyone in Berlin had »discovered« her long before I came along.

Her past history was of no importance to me, and I told her that. Taking note that I was not easily discouraged, the lady now informed me that she had seen some of my previous work, and though she reluctantly conceded that I knew how to handle men she doubted that I could do as well with women. As I was now face to face with a critic, I offered to make a test of her to prove that she could be photographed properly, and that I had talent enough not to fumble when confronted by the female of the species. Before agreeing to this, she made a condition that I must first look at the last three films which had featured her.

The next day proved to be an ordeal. If I had first seen her films before seeing her on the stage, my reaction would have been the same as everyone else's. In them she was an awkward, unattractive woman, left to her own devices, and presented in an embarrassing exhibition of drivel. Ice-cold water was poured on me. In any event I dreaded tests. I had made only two of them before. A director making a test either takes what is placed before the camera and allows the mechanism to take its toll, or the instrument is used to record whether the human being in front of it can be guided by him; whether the actor lights up into a bright flame or is extinguished. My brand of fuel had often inflamed an actor, not so much because some of it landed on him but because I was thought to be too liberal with it, wasting it on everything else within range. Few are aware of the contribution made by the apparently invisible to the visible. To photograph a human being properly, all that surrounds him must definitely add to him, or it will do nothing but subtract.

I was always inclined to ration the little fuel that

was mine to spray, saving it for when it was needed, rather than wasting it on tests that could mean nothing. Of the two tests I had made, one was of Ruth Chatterton, and it had helped her to stardom; in the other I had allowed the mechanism to take its toll. This was a test of a famous acting group known as the Habima players, who had visited Hollywood. I was asked not to guide them in any manner, merely to allow them to express themselves, as they were loaded with talent to which no one could make a contribution. I was only to see to it that their demonstration of acting finesse would not be lost by the camera. This proved to be not quite so easy as had been anticipated. The cameraman threw me a glance of desperation and I took over the control of the mobile tripod mount to keep the performers from eluding the lens. Theirs was the agility of rabbits. I managed to swing the turret in time to follow one giant leap as an actress about to hurtle through the air was nailed to the floor by a nimble fellow actor, who seized her by the throat and bellowed »*Prostitutke!*« before the others attacked to pry him loose in a witches' sabbath of acrobatic histrionics. This was to have been a courtesy test to be presented to this able group by M-G-M, but it would have been a greater courtesy not to have made a permanent record of that bedlam.

In the case of Fräulein Dietrich, the problem was not one of being able to follow wild movements but of persuading her to make any movement. (Incidentally, she was not a Fräulein but a Frau, as she was a married woman.*) I first limbered up by making a test of the organization's chief contender for the part I wished to bestow on my choice. This candidate was a charming, witty young woman by the name of Lucie Mannheim, who appeared with a talented musician to play the piano for her. Though both impressed me, it was the musician, Friedrich Hollander, whom I retained to work with me on the composition of the music and songs for the film.

Following this test, Frau Dietrich appeared. She had not prepared herself in any way, for she thought the entire matter a waste of time. So did I, as I had made up my mind to use her, though she did not know this. In her own coy version, now a solid part of her legend, she claims to have been a drama student in the Reinhardt school* when I noticed her, and in some of her interviews she has stated that I asked her to sing a vulgar song for the test, though in her stage act she claims that the song that she was asked to sing was merely »naughty.« While it is entirely possible that she may have attended the school, it is impossible that I ever asked anyone to be vulgar. As for my asking her to sing a »naughty« song for the test, this too is not to be reconciled with what actually happened. As she had made no preparation for the test and had brought no pianist with her, she could only sing what she knew, and that was very little. I sent her to the wardrobe to discard her street clothes and to change into something with spangles and she returned with a costume roomy enough to contain a hippopotamus. I pinned the dress to fit her somehow and asked her to sing something she knew in German and to follow it with an English song if possible.

I then put her into the crucible of my conception, blended her image to correspond with mine, and, pouring lights on her until the alchemy was complete, proceeded with the test. She came to life and responded to my instructions with an ease that I had never before encountered. She seemed pleased at the trouble I took with her, but she never saw the test, nor ever asked to see it. Her remarkable vitality had been channeled.

The two tests were screened the following morning in a crowded projection room. A unanimous opinion ruled out the woman of my choice in favor of Lucie Mannheim. I could not credit my ears, for the screen gave full proof of a unique personality. Everyone connected with the making of the film was present, and, according to a custom more prevalent, the room was also filled with others who had no knowledge of what was planned. All of them opposed my preference. Finally a prominent fellow director, Hans Schwarz, rose portentously to state that it was ridiculous to choose between the two as everyone with eyes in his head could see the superiority of Miss Mannheim. I thanked him for confirming my judgment. In the silence that

---

* Her name was Frau Sieber.

* I was present when later she told Max Reinhardt that she had attended his school. His eyebrows did not resume their normal position for almost twenty minutes.

followed my sarcasm, Erich Pommer quietly settled the matter by stating that the choice of the cast was my responsibility and that it was his responsibility to support me. This of course was the final word, except for one more small voice that came from Emil Jannings, who muttered in a hollow voice that would have brought credit to Cassandra that I would rue the day.

The cast of players was now complete, and the filming began. My leading lady had been engaged for a relatively small sum, though the five thousand dollars her contract called for was almost a hundred times as much as the pittance she earned at the theatre, where she had to appear nightly throughout the entire filming. In a short time, to jump ahead, her earning power became phenomenal. But there was no thought of the future while she was in my film; her hours were too full to think ahead. She had to be at the studio at seven in the morning and work late until she barely had time to reach her theatre for the night performance; after which, so I was told, she went to a midnight dinner with her friends to regale them with a vivid and explicit account of what she was forced to endure on my stages. Normally this hearsay trivia would not be worth recounting except that it is in quaint contrast to the praise she chose to extend later. During the filming she complained that what I was instructing her to do would make it impossible for her to ever show her face again, repeating this even after she saw the completed film. At the time she told others that her torture was not only intensified by the twists and turns her body was subjected to but that each sound from her came under directorial censure. This foreigner, who ruled the stage with an iron hand, not only made her speak an English that had vowels and consonants that were beyond belief but he even had the temerity to assume jurisdiction over her native language. It was punishing enough to work with Jannings, who, though the prime consideration of the director, was notorious for his tantrums, but, worst of all, she could do nothing to please this other exacting person, and if that was the way to make a living she would have none of it.

Some of this more or less normal litany might well be justified. So far as Jannings was concerned, it was not easy to work with him. Far from unaware of what other actors were contributing, he watched her respond to me with uncommon delight, though he drew a veil of scorn over his eyes when the scene was over, and he did attempt to interfere with her performance. But that was all the evidence I had that she was not having a wonderful time. Her behavior on my stage was a marvel to behold. Her attention was riveted on me. No property master could have been more alert. She behaved as if she were there as my servant, first to notice that I was looking about for a pencil, first to rush for a chair when I wanted to sit down. Not the slightest resistance was offered to my domination of her performance. Rarely did I have to take a scene with her more than once. Perhaps I failed to praise her and was, as is my nature, a trifle too critical, but she along with others saw each day's work in the projection room, though it is possible that in seeing segments few persons can appraise the ultimate effect.

Parenthetically, my reluctance to be indiscriminate with praise, such as might have made her task and that of the others easier, calls for explanation. The nature of our work is such that each step has to be weighed in terms of the involved expense. There is no allocation in the budget for pondering or reconsidering anything a director does. My work can rarely please me, for it consists of a series of concessions to myself and to others. If a scene does not turn out to correspond to my inner vision, the time at my disposal to change it is extremely limited, for only after I have succeeded in making the actors conform to the preliminary requirements am I in a position to assess the possible effectiveness of what was planned. A film is made under conditions that assume the director knows at all times what is best for all concerned. This is absurd; there is no one whose every step can be correct. Day after day goes by in making small sections of film, often unrelated to each other, and the cohesion, the flow, and most important of all, the abstract values to be released become evident only when the segments have been subjected to the manipulation of scissors and glue. Nothing that takes place is automatic or even orderly. And over every move hovers the spectre of a future audience that must be ensnared or it might prevent one from ever making another film. The Mongolian who dismounts from his dusty camel to exchange his fifty *mung* for a look-see at the film may be the final arbiter. This is not an exaggeration – his equivalent can be found in every theatre.

A film is not like an automobile, though it may have as many parts. A frame is made to contain the performer. A background is evoked, each ray of light aids or detracts, foreground is interposed, the very air becomes part of the effect. The performer is charged to dig beneath his consciousness to surface something unstale and rare. What emerges may have to be rejected. And what takes place on the stage is not the all-important factor. The search for values is not limited to what is visible to the lens. The material must be processed, image and sound made to conform to a pattern that has no chart. From beginning to end it is nothing but an improvisation. The result must be edited long after the work on the stages is done, compressed and stretched to a cadence only dimly apparent. How does one burst into applause and praise the performer every time he breathes? Often enough, my comment after a scene consists of »Well, let's try the next one.« It is no aid to a grown-up to be treated like a child.

Anyway, the agony which the woman who was to become famous said she had to endure lasted about six weeks. There are two ways of measuring the length of an agony, if such it was. One is to compare it with the span of the fame that follows; the other is to perceive that six weeks of agony can seem endless. There was also a period of waiting before the filming began, and many weeks of tense waiting afterward while I sat in a room hunched over a clattering machine through which passed the miles of celluloid that represented our labors. The making of a film is a slow process which many have tried to speed up. I am reminded of the neat anecdote about the impatient surgeon, anxious to operate, who was irritated by the methodical preparations of his anaesthetist. »Aren't you extremely slow?« he finally said. The man, who was taking his time, replied, »There is this way, and a still slower way.«

However, the creation of a new film star, an incidental by-product of *The Blue Angel,* was not slow. No one, certainly not the »incidental by-product« herself, was aware that so swift and dramatic a transformation from a comparative nonentity to an international celebrity had been accomplished. Even the Ufa officials, after seeing the completed film, were not aware of it, for they did not exercise an option on the future services of Frau Dietrich, an option that had been carefully included in her contract. This was an obvious blunder, for the retention of a prominent player on a company's roster is more than a necessity for its existence. But to be fair to the executives of this now relatively unimportant organization, and in particular, to Erich Pommer, who was able and farsighted, this phase of their work was not what was bothering them. What concerned them was that a German film had been made by a non-German, and that to them the film did not seem to be German. The details that permeated the film had no relation to the strict school system of Germany, and the entire idea of a German professor going wenching in defiance of propriety was more than obnoxious. The outward picture of German pride and morality had been violated, and a storm of protest from the public and authorities was expected.

In spite of their perhaps well-founded fears, some erudite writers subsequently said that the film was a true representation of the time in which it was made. For instance, Siegfried Kracauer in his *From Caligari to Hitler,* labeling it a »study in sadism,« refers to it as a »considered statement of the psychological situation of the time.« Going far afield, he mentions that the pupils I presented are »born Hitler youths and the cockcrowing device is a modest contribution to a group of similar, if more ingenious contrivances used in Nazi concentration camps.« I must be forgiven if I state once more that most of the story of the film and its details existed only in my imagination, that I knew very little about Germany before I began it, that then I had not yet seen anyone resembling a Nazi, and that the entire stimulation to make the film came from a book that was written by Heinrich Mann in the good old days before 1905.

In Cannes the Pasha of Marrakech once asked me why I had not visited him while in his domain. I told him I would have paid my respects had I ever been in Morocco, whereupon he said he had seen a film of mine and that it contained scenes photographed on streets that he recognized. He smiled when I told him that this was no more than an accidental resemblance, a flaw due to my lack of talent to avoid such similarity. To make this point once more: in another film made with a Russian locale, I asked a Russian whether the Russians behaved as they did in my film. »No,« he answered, »they do not, but they should.«

And this actual lack of resemblance to the reality also bothered the actress who had been »tormented« into my image of her. She had fashioned a woman who had no existence except on the screen. This distressed her. She had not yet changed, though there were some minor portents that she was not the same actress I had seen on the stage barely two months before. While I was still at work putting together the pieces of what turned out to be a celluloid monument for her, she complained that the advance notices had concentrated on me and the great Emil, barely mentioning her. She was beginning to confuse the quality of a performance with the size of the name of the performer. Regardless of her conviction that the film just being assembled would ruin her forever, she wanted that ruin to be properly publicized. I could do nothing about this, as this was not my province, though I told her that her name would become better known than anyone else's in the film.

This was swiftly followed by another indication that she had taken new stock of herself. I had shown the initial test made of her to Mr. Ben Schulberg, who had visited Berlin, and he had followed my advice and cabled her quite a generous offer to come to Hollywood. Though they were not, she thought the salary provisions absurd. As I remember it, this annoyed me. I recall rather vaguely that I showed her my watch and told her I would give her five minutes to make up her mind whether or not she wanted to make another film with me, and in Hollywood.

Though she has subsequently disputed this, I have a faint recollection that the watch was torn from my grasp and flung away. I was wrong, of course. Five minutes is not time enough to consider the severance of connections with country, family, friends, and language. Early the next morning my lady brought a bouquet of mimosa to my workroom, and soon thereafter I left Germany to return to my California home, not expecting to see her again. I had churned up an ocean, and up had come a woman who was to charm the world.

There are not only two sides to every story but close to a thousand, and the chances are that not one of them is completely trustworthy. One side of the story that concerns my relationship with Frau Dietrich has long ago been told with the camera in seven films, and it would not surprise me if it were least trustworthy of all. The intention here is not to tell another version but to assess the tools of our craft and to clarify their elastic and elusive characteristics. The tools are human, and the workman wielding them is human too. The motion picture is only a highly developed shadow play, and to manipulate human beings as if they were puppets made of the hide of water buffaloes is to ask for trouble.

As the *Bremen* pushed itself away from the shores of Germany I watched the receding docks and turned to my assistant to say, »I'm glad that's over. Let's hope that nobody follows me.« This is the strongest memory I have of that period, though memory consists only of the things we wish to remember.

On the eve of April Fool's Day, 1930, *The Blue Angel* was unrolled before the Berlin public for the first time. Erich Pommer, with a discretion rare among producers in the annals of our profession, had let my work speak for itself, not tampering with a single frame.* By coincidence or not, that very evening was the time for Frau Dietrich to leave for Hollywood, since she had decided to accept the Paramount contract. The railroad station was close to the Gloria Palast where the film opened, and as the boat train was not scheduled to leave until midnight, she had been persuaded to take a bow at the finish of the performance that she thought would bring her ruin and oblivion. It is pleasant to record that she was not attired as if she might have to sneak out of the stage door and run for the waiting train, but was festooned and garlanded in the flouncy tradition of a film star. She received a thunderous ovation. The beginning of the journey into the stratosphere had been nicely timed.

Cables from my associates notified me how the film had been received by public and critics. But not so the cable that came from a ship. It merely read: »Who is to play opposite me?« I replied that Gary Cooper had been chosen, though it was not what I was tempted to reply. Added to the ordi-

---

*Though mentioned before, I repeat it here, for it constitutes one of the most flagrant abuses in our craft.

nary difficulties of my work, an actress had been launched in a few hasty weeks who would now play a part that had not been written for her. »He that is surety for a stranger shall smart for it« is proclaimed by the Old Testament.

A stranger she was, for no one had seen *The Blue Angel* outside Germany, and it was not shown in the United States until she had once more revealed herself as a stellar attraction in the second film made under my »tormenting« tutelage. This post-graduation piece was to be named *Morocco*. Miss Dietrich had much more to do with the choice of this second vehicle than merely conforming to the instructions of her teacher, for when I had left Berlin, before I knew that she would follow, she had sent a *bon voyage* basket to the ship, and in it was a novel by Benno Vigny. Its title was *Amy Jolly*, and it dealt with the Foreign Legion. As I read it in an idle moment, it occurred to me that there was a foreign legion of women, so to speak, who also chose to hide their wounds behind an incognito.

Upon being informed that this book was to be the basis for the next film, she had cabled that it would be better to chose a more suitable story for her, protesting that *Amy Jolly* was »schwache Limonade« (»weak lemonade«). Her judgment was correct so far as the subject matter of the novel was concerned, for she could not possibly know the reason for its choice. I had deliberately selected a theme that was visual and owed no allegiance to a cascade of words. Not only was I aware of the importance of maintaining the international force of the medium and its appeal to distant peoples, most of whom had a vocabulary not exceeding five hundred words, but my selection had been influenced by a practical consideration.

I had shuddered at the idea of the sounds that would emerge from the mouth of my Aphrodite when the time came to engage in mortal combat with an unfamiliar language. Her German and French were impeccable, but her knowledge of English was then poor, and unless carefully handled, difficult to reconcile with the charm of her looks. Weber and Fields and their many successors had made audiences howl with their imitations of English slaughtered by the German novice. An image that had no accent, German or otherwise, could not be subjected to a guttural pronunciation with rolling r sounds, v substituted for w, ch for j, b for p and z for s. My fears were not based on any fantasy, for in filming the English version of *The Blue Angel* simultaneously with the German, I had witnessed the facial contortions and the wrestling match with the tongue that went with the most elemental sounds that came from her lips. Plainly she would need to be kept out of sight until this handicap was overcome, though there was no way of concealing her in a film which was to feature her.

When she arrived in Hollywood it proved to be impossible to keep her hidden from the press, especially its feminine section, eager to evaluate what had been imported. I urged her to refrain from practicing her English on the press, but lacked the sense not to practice mine also. At a luncheon, arranged to introduce Frau Dietrich to the Hollywood magazine scribes, I indulged in a stupid remark which stung the women present, and as if I had attacked a school of cuttlefish, the ladies discharged their ink at me. To quote: »›And besides all this‹, he said in closing, ›she has that quality rare in women – brains.‹« This sally caused quite a commotion. I had no qualification to make such a statement, knowing few women and very little about that part of female anatomy.

The indignation at her silence was parceled out to me. She was the modest little German *Hausfrau* and I was the villain who would not allow her to speak or to appear in public. But as her work was not known, the initial interest soon subsided, and I was able to concentrate on the preparations for the film in which this unknown was to make her appearance.

The stages were made ready, the sand dunes of the Sahara were found in California, and we covered a few dusty roads in nearby San Fernando Valley with overhead trellises and palm leaves, and lined one of them with skulls mounted on sticks to provide for the entry of a company of Legionnaires. Next in line were the uniforms and the costumes for the leading lady.

I had seen the »modest little German *Hausfrau*,« whom all these preparations were to frame, wearing the full-dress regalia of a man, high hat and all, at a Berlin shindy, and so outfitted her, planning to have her dress like a man in one of the café sequences when she would sing in French and, circulating among the audience, favor another woman with a kiss. The formal male finery fitted her with much charm, and I not only wished to touch lightly on a Lesbian accent (no scene of mine having any sexual connotation has ever been censored) but also to demonstrate that her sensual appeal was not entirely due to the classic formation of her legs. Having her wear trousers was not meant to stimulate a fashion which not long after the film was shown encouraged women to ignore skirts in favor of the less picturesque lower half of male attire.

Asked to make a trailer to acquaint the sales force with a potential star, she appeared in a short scene wearing white tie and tails. At once I ran into a storm of opposition. The studio officials swore by all that was sacred that their wives wore nothing but skirts, one of them even going so far as to claim that a pair of trousers could not be lifted. Hours of debate ensued, draining my energies and theirs. While they could recuperate, I would be making the film, and their opinion seemed to be that a director needed no energy to do his work. When I stood my ground on the question of what my performers were going to wear, the choice of the players became a bone of contention. Gary Cooper was considered to be harmless enough not to injure the film, but Adolphe Menjou was turned down as a liability until it was pointed out that all this was of no importance as the film had to sink or swim solely on the merits of an unknown personality. In passing, it should be mentioned that less than a year later Adolph Zukor confided to me that the company had been saved from bankruptcy by the success of this film.

It was finally conceded that the debonair Menjou could join the cast, and so this gentleman became privileged to share in the opening scenes of *Morocco*, with which I hoped to repeat what had been done once before – the transformation of my protégée into a star.

We had bad luck at the very beginning. The scenario describes the opening scene as taking place on the forward deck of a small steamer approaching the shore of North Africa. Leaning on the rail, peering into the foggy night that shrouds her destination, is a mysterious woman, her forlorn countenance made luminous by a beam of light aimed at her by one of my electricians. Normally the men who manipulate the lights recline on the scaffolding, reading comics or dozing, fairly indifferent to what transpires below them. But not this time. Their eyes were pinned on someone unknown to them who had aroused their curiosity, for the director seemed to be taking excessive pains, gauzing and masking light rays to toy with her skin texture, even asking for a »cucaracha« (a transparent plastic contraption with broken surface) in order to bounce a few highlights here and there. And whereas most featured players had substitutes standing in for light adjustments, this lady waited without a sign of impatience for the director to signal the beginning of the scene.

The director then took his place behind the camera and an assistant called, »Scene one, take one.« Jauntily, Mr. Menjou, playing a citizen of the world, strolled by an assortment of Arabs and Levantines sprawling on the deck to accost the inscrutable female gazing intently into the dark, her eyes riveted on a board on which had been chalked »North Africa.« Raising his hat, he stated politely that he knew the country ahead and asked whether he could be of any help. So far, so good – everything was going along well. Then the scene required that the woman being photographed as an alluring enigma look him up and down in sober appraisal while the muffled foghorn moaned. She was to reject his kind offer by saying that she needed no help, but she was to voice this in a way to indicate that her immediate destiny was a dubious one.

The words were »I don't need any help.« That was what was put in, but it was not what came out. The star of my film, in the first sounds designed to enrapture an audience, had taken one of the words of that simple sentence into her mouth and garbled it. Everyone was startled, even Mr. Menjou, whose poise was proverbial; but more than startled was the man at the sound controls, who threw me a despairing look like a trout about to expire. The word »help« had been mutilated to sound like »hellubh.«

Unaffected, I approached from behind the camera and explained to the lady, who had failed to take note of the commotion her linguistics had aroused, that there was nothing unusual about a first take being unsatisfactory, that the scene would be more effective were excess syllables eliminated. I carefully called attention to the fact that »help« contained only four letters and needed no additional sounds to make it intelligible. She listened carefully, as she always did, and mentioned that she might never be able to discard an accent. With this I agreed, but I stated that the accent would have to be acceptable to me.

After a few more attempts on her part to embellish a simple word with sounds that would have made a laughingstock of both of us, I suggested that she substitute the word »assistance« for the word that gave her so much trouble. This, after a few preliminary trial runs through the teeth, she declined to consider, saying that the other word was preferable. By this time the stage was in a dither. Various bystanders were melting away, and couriers had been dispatched to every department in the studio to inform them that all was not as it should be.

We tried it a few more times, the result being the same and aggravated by additional stumbles due to the tension. Her sharp ears had taken note of an alien sound that preceded the letter *l*, and she reproduced the sound formed by the movement of the tongue to expel that letter to the best of her ability. Suggestions were made by my solicitous staff members. Why not approve the scene as good enough and, on a later day, when the word could be properly pronounced, record it and then insert it into the sound track? This procedure would have been quite normal, but was out of the question in this case, for if this portion of the film were to be seen the following morning by the studio executives, who inspected each day's work as if it were representative of the entire film, the German charmer would promptly be eliminated from the project. No, this was the acid test!

This had become not a challenge to achieve perfection, neither was it a problem of recording a sentence that was acceptable enough, for I could always have a foghorn blow at the critical point so that no one could notice the destructive pronunciation that dealt a deathblow to her charm. This had now become a question of whether or not I could direct her. Pictorially she was more than effective, and it was obvious that she was eager to conform to my guidance; there was not the slightest impatience visible in her bearing, but what sort of a performance could she give if a foghorn blew whenever she opened her mouth?

I persisted in the attempt to teach her how to pronounce the fatal word. Though a pallor had now spread over the faces of those who had remained on the stage, she was unperturbed. She knew that there was something wrong, and she had seen this sort of thing during the making of her first film with me, participating with others in having pronunciation and tone corrected, and in the German language as well as in English. Concluding that perhaps my enunciation was at fault, Menjou was asked to pronounce the word for her several times, and when that failed, others were told to drop the fateful word into her ear. Each time, in went the word »help«, out came vowels, consonants, and an occasional diphthong that failed to meet any known standard of charm. My patience with actors is not limited except by their endurance, and hour after hour fled. The fact that I had to speak German to her made matters worse, for nobody had the slightest idea of what was being done to improve matters. Menjou, who had a smattering of German, had retired, pleading a headache.

Suddenly I had an inspiration. I instructed the young lady who had endured all this without a whimper to pronounce the letters *h-e-l-p* in German and to forget that it was an English word. Out came the word, this time faultlessly. The scene was recorded without further incident, and the launching of the good ship Marlene was under way. On that foul day my reputation as one of the swiftest directors in films was dealt quite a blow.

The viewpoint of the company that chose to tolerate the manner in which I worked is not to be ignored. I was an employee, not free to do as I pleased or to be highhanded. Though others might have thought me out of line, I considered my work to be solely my responsibility. The organization was being presented with an international stellar attraction, under contract to it (not to me) – an asset that helped to keep the company solvent for a while. Nothing could save it permanently, for no large film company can survive the wasteful system under which it operates. There is no such thing as a production line for talent.

My contribution to the company's temporary success was acknowledged by its chief executive at the premiere of *Morocco*. Sitting next to me, he nudged me, saying, »Look at them eating it up. They think they're seeing a big picture.« But during the making of the film his nudging was of a different caliber. While working in a temperature of one hundred and twenty degrees Fahrenheit, dodging real estate signs and telegraph poles that could not possibly help to suggest North Africa, I received a memorandum from him stating that unless I worked faster he would replace me. Later that evening I phoned him to ask how fast he wanted me to work. Impatient, because a game of poker had been interrupted, he answered, »Never mind how fast, just get a move on.« I countered by informing him that the schedule for the film was a meager five weeks, and that I was not behind schedule. Aiming his voice away from the mouthpiece toward the table from which came shouts for him to rejoin the game, he bellowed: »I have no time to discuss details. Work faster or we switch directors.«* This was a common threat. In their impotence, aside from their unquestionable power to hire and fire, most executives were not only switching all that they could switch but being switched themselves, though rarely replaced by anyone more capable. The history of a film studio is like the history of the guillotine: each head is followed in turn by the head that had arranged the previous decapitation.

More pertinent to this inquiry is the viewpoint of the immediate beneficiaries of my labors. It has been stated before that women seem to be less resentful of outright manipulation than men. But the case of the woman who emerged as the star of *Morocco* presents some curious aspects. Not only was she less resentful than others might have been but she went to extremes in praising the director who forced her to submit to constant inspection and guidance. During her first film with me in Berlin, when she was unimportant and no one outside of her immediate circle took notice of her, it was easy to complain that nothing on earth was worth such torture. But those who had listened so eagerly before might not be so sympathetic to her woes following the unique success her woes had brought on. All Europe was at her feet, and with the impact of her appearance in *Morocco*, her fame had spread to where it no longer could be confined to one continent.

* Addressing a group of writers, Mr. Schulberg, who was a ready wit, remarked: »Now is a bad time for you writers to be making demands, just when the whole industry is bending every effort to make the world safe for von Sternberg.« – N.Y. *Evening Journal*, April 28, 1932.

Enthusiastic reviews poured in, her fan mail kept an entire department on its feet, her photographs were now requested, men wished to lay their fortunes at her feet, and celebrities vied with each other to be seen and photographed with her. Tribute was collected from men of rank and fame, the most famous actors wished to have her as their partner, producers and directors couldn't wait until they could work with her, and her circle increased to include the top writers and creators of her day. Dukes and generals and even the heads of nations wanted her to grace their tables. One journalist, quoted in one of the many books devoted to her, not only raved about her beauty but »rated her brains on a par with those of Napoleon, Caesar, Mussolini and Lenin.«*

Opposed to this pinnacle of glory was her position on my stage. Here was no enthusiast, but a cold-eyed mechanic critical of every movement. If there was any flattery, it was concentrated in a »That's fine, it will do.« More often she listened to »Turn your shoulders away from me and straighten out... Drop your voice an octave and don't lisp... Count to six and look at that lamp as if you could no longer live without it... Stand where you are and don't move; the lights are being adjusted.«

How is it possible for a mortal to balance adulation of the most profligate sort with the apparently cruel submission required to retain that admiration? This quasi slavery is not secret, for it takes place on an open stage and can be witnessed by a hundred eyes. She had only to step beyond the range of the lights to be greeted enthusiastically by an avid press. It is extremely difficult to find adjustment to this abnormal contrast.

She now retailed her »torments« not as a complaint, but managed to turn this by shrewd indirection into an outstanding virtue. She flipped the other side of the coin, and with commendable instinct turned herself into a martyr who praised the divine grace which favored her with lacerations. She told everyone who would listen – and there were few who would not – that I let her walk out into a blazing desert, barefooted, and would not stop her after the scene had been completed because I had just enough sunlight to make one more

* This quote is attributed to journalist C. H. Rand by Leslie Frewin in his book *Blonde Venus* (London, Macgibbon & Kee, 1955).

scene in which she was not needed, and that when she had fainted from exhaustion and been carried back to lie at my feet I corrected her English when she had recovered enough to ask if I required another close-up. This was not said to inform anyone that she had been mistreated. On the contrary, it was twisted into a form of praise for me. »Isn't he wonderful? He even corrects my English when I don't come out of a fainting spell properly.«

This mixture of self-abasement leavened with praise for me, this concoction of crawling submission to a mentor, took effect at once. In the beginning the defensive maneuver was most probably an instinctive measure, if it was not genuine humility, but as soon as it was evident that it produced additional admiration, there was no good reason to refrain from earning a few plaudits on her own account. No one could take umbrage at paying tribute to another. A geyser of praise began to shoot, hot and steaming, on the hour and every hour, and there was nothing I could do to avoid being scalded.

It was not long before I could tell even from a distance whom she had favored with her eulogies by noting a venomous look thrown at me. She complained of being guided exactly as did all the others, though the form in which she stated her complaint varied. This pupil, like all the others, groaned. In her case the complaint was made obliquely, but it was the same lament. »Oh, what we must suffer for the sake of God's church!« as the abbot exclaimed when he singed the skin of his fingers on the roast fowl.

The suffering of an actor, to call attention once more to this seemingly unavoidable vicissitude, is self-inflicted, due entirely to the precarious nature of his services. And when, as sometimes happens, the director's contribution is too effective to be ignored, the wound already there festers, even though the director has been as aseptic as it is possible for him to be. ...

So here I am, between Scylla and Charybdis. On one hand excessive fulmination, on the other destructive flummery. As the voice of the charming woman discovered by me became stronger in extolling her director, the slander in opposition to her »praise« became thunderous. The scale always remained in balance. »Poor little me, I had nothing to do with this, and look how wonderful this scene is when I'm not even in it,« only sparked a detonation that backfired on me. Cartoons and films made capital of all this blurbing, and plays were written in which caricatures were perpetrated, supposedly based on antics of mine. There was nothing I could do to combat the nursery tales that followed in the wake of my work.

As the only casualty resulting from creating *The Blue Angel* and *Morocco* was my reputation as a considerate workman, I proceeded with a third film featuring the lady of my choice. This was based on a story of mine called »X 27.« It dealt with a Viennese streetwalker whose services are enlisted in an espionage system. The company decided to title the film *Dishonored,* disregarding my protest that the lady spy was not dishonored but killed by a firing squad. Again my lovely charmer, now fully established as the reigning queen of the cinema, disclaimed credit for her performance, and once more this ricocheted and gained additional laurels for her, sprinkled with abuse for the director. The film contained some interesting experiments in visual and tonal effects, one of them even recognized by the Academy of Motion Picture Arts and Sciences, which bestowed a statuette on the studio's sound department for something to which they had strongly objected. The execution of the female spy was staged in a balloon hangar with its echoing sounds, an improvised stage disapproved by the sound mechanics, who refused to take responsibility for what they were ordered to record.

Then the star of *The Blue Angel, Morocco,* and *Dishonored* returned to Europe to recover from her arduous labors, while I took a rest doing a little finger exercise on *An American Tragedy.* ...

The lady indirectly responsible for this accolade now returned from Germany where she had become a legendary figure. She was no legend to me. I had made up my mind to stop painting the lily, and I told her so. But I had not anticipated her reaction to my wish not to use her again. She accused me of being determined to demonstrate to all and sundry that she was worthless, to aggrandize myself by letting her stand on her own feet; she was nothing and could do nothing without me, and all I had done with her was only to show how great I was.

What I proposed was out of the question! She refused to work with another director. The organization to which we both were under contract also came to bat and demanded that I continue to guide her. The studio's top official,* a new one this time, literally went down on his knees to beg me not to get him into trouble by abandoning a valuable asset. I agreed to continue, as I had no wish to harm anyone, least of all the woman for whom I felt myself responsible.

In a pedantic history of the motion picture by two erudite Frenchmen, Bardèche and Brasillach, with annotations by Iris Barry, presumably selected for alliterative reasons, my contribution to the art of films during the days to follow is carefully appraised:

»There followed a succession of deplorable films, each one more lavish and stupider than the others, in which this magnificent creature, Marlene Dietrich, laden with feathers and jewels, became a mere clotheshorse. The director made the welkin ring with his oaths and disputes as he continually vowed he would have nothing more to do with such a fiend, yet returning to her again and again, losing his skill at film making apparently forever.«**

Of course this was written before others, whose skill was rarely questioned, made films with my »fiend.« Many of these films are forgotten, though the talented directors included Ernst Lubitsch, Rouben Mamoulian, Frank Borzage, Richard Boleslavski, Jacques Feyder, George Marshall, Tay Garnett, René Clair, Raoul Walsh, Mitchell Leisen, Ray Enright, Lewis Seiler, Edward Sutherland, Wilhelm Dieterle, Henry Koster, Frank Lloyd, Fritz Lang, Orson Welles, Alfred Hitchcock, Billy Wilder, Georges Lacombe, Michael Anderson, Samuel Taylor, Stanley Kramer, and others.

The aforementioned quotation, dealing with my work with this exceptional woman, is only one of the more moderate examples that abound in textbooks recommended at the university level for deep insight into the mechanics of making a film. Though these films and others of mine are constantly hauled out of the vaults to be shown at retrospectives in many parts of the world, the literature concerning them wastes no space dealing with the content and instead revolves sagely around a fabled character trumped up to be me. . . . Having survived *An American Tragedy,* I continued to »gloat lovingly« on the next theme »repugnant to the normal mind.« This repulsive subject concerned the journey of a train from Peking to Shanghai. A China was built of papier-mâché and into it we placed slant-eyed men, women, and children, who seemed to relish being part of it. We borrowed a train from the Santa Fe, painted it white, and added an armored car to carry Chinese soldiers with fixed bayonets. To convey what organizing film detail comprises, we had to plan to have a cow give birth and nourish its calf near noisy railroad tracks, so that it would be undisturbed by clanging bells and hooting whistles when my train came along through the crowded streets to be stopped by an animal suckling its young.

But, as everyone knows, it is easier to outguess animals than to predict the behavior of human beings. Though Shanghai Lily was not permitted by me to expose either leg or ankle, the pattern of discriminating film criticism had by this time been established. *Vanity Fair,* then the unquestioned mouthpiece of the intelligentsia, worked me over with:

»He traded his open style for fancy play, chiefly upon the legs in silk, and buttocks in lace, of Dietrich, of whom he has made a paramount slut. By his own token, Sternberg is a man of meditation as well as a man of action; but instead of contemplating the navel of Buddha his umbilical perseverance is fixed on the navel of Venus.«*

Into the fray also came Tovarich Eisenstein, who called my *Shanghai Express* a »Kiddy-Kar« version of a Russian film he had seen. Thus the oboe and the bassoon.

There also were some flutes, though the less said about them the better. Ayn Rand told me that rarely had any film so impressed her, and when I asked her why she thought so, she spoke of a scene that was unforgettable to her: »The way the wind blows through the fur-piece around Marlene's shoulder when she sits on the back platform of the train!« Another keen observer, Mr. William

---

* Emanuel Cohn.
** New York, W. W. Norton & Co., Inc., and Museum of Modern Art, 1938.

* March, 1932.

FitzGerald, who wrote an entire book on my work, had this to say: »If von Sternberg did not turn his lens to the star's legs, he did observe that she possessed beautiful hands and he put his knowledge to advantage in the sequence where the heroine prays alone in the darkness.«

Though my performers could not respond to my instructions with the same speed as the train which contained them, I thought the canvas of China, as evoked by my imagination, quite effective. The film, loosely based on a single page by Harry Hervey, featured a hold-up by bandits. This caused the Chinese to resent the slur on their national law and order, and they banned the film wherever they could, and I was told that if ever I appeared in China I would be arrested and punished. Nevertheless, some years later I managed to enter that extraordinary country, after the train that brought me there was delayed by bandits soon after crossing the Manchurian border.

The actual Shanghai Express, which I then took out of Peking, was thoroughly unlike the train I had invented, except that it, too, carried a protecting complement of armed military. I was more than pleased that I had delineated a China before being confronted with its vast and variegated reality.* There is quite a difference between fact and fancy.

I became more and more partial to fancy as I proceeded to make a fifth film with my fair lady in another vehicle deemed unworthy of her superb talents. One writer stated it thus: »It is as if the Delphic Oracle had stepped down from her pedestal to give her opinion of the weather.« This film was *Blonde Venus,* also based on a story of mine written swiftly to provide something other than the sob stories that were being submitted. There is little to be said about this film, except that I tried to leave the company before making it. But Miss Dietrich also left, refusing to work with anyone else, and I was forced to return, as we were both under contract. I remember this opus very vaguely, but recalled some of it years later while driving through France with a charming companion who, in a moment of confidence, after we had stopped in Rouen for goose and Beaujolais, leaned toward me to say, »You know, it took me five years to understand what you said to me when I worked in your film.« This was Cary Grant, whom I had rescued from a status as one of Mae West's foils to launch him on his stellar career. After all, five years is not too long a time to understand what someone else is trying to impart.

At the close of this fifth film with Marlene I managed to persuade her finally to try a film with another director, and while I went on a vacation Rouben Mamoulian took her in hand to make *Song of Songs.* I did not see this film but saw a statue of her used in the film which showed her in the nude.

I returned to the treadmill to make the last two of the seven films with her. These last two, in which I completely subjugated my bird of paradise to my peculiar tendency to prove that a film might well be an art medium, were not bad, but audience and critics turned thumbs down. I took note of that with deep regret. *The Scarlet Empress,* the penultimate film, deserved to be successful by any standard then existing or now prevalent, but with few exceptions it was greeted as an attempt to assassinate a superb actress. The film was, of course, a relentless excursion into style, which, taken for granted in any work of art, is considered to be unpardonable in this medium. The tapestry of the Russia of Catherine the Great was evoked in all its grandeur, though it was a re-creation and not a replica. The story of the rise of a guileless young princess to a mocking and ruthless empress could not be dull even if it were derailed for a moment to show a locket of her faithless lover falling from branch to branch of a wintry tree to dangle for a second before it drops into the snow. As the now enraged gentlemen of the jury pointed out, every single scene bore my imprint.

Mea culpa; I had not left much for others to do, even being bold enough to conduct the members of the Los Angeles Symphony orchestra in playing the background music. During one of the sessions a cellist made some extraneous noise and he was asked what his notes read at that point. He replied, »*Tacet,*« and I told him to stick to his notes. The press was jubilant!**Here was final proof that this

---

* George Amberg, who teaches Theatre of the Absurd at the University of Minnesota, recently told me that he had written a paper on the Fetish of Authenticity. I consider this a noteworthy concentration of a theme in a title.

** The article deriding me for apparently not knowing the meaning of *tacet* was in *The Hollywood Reporter,* June 23, 1934.

man knew nothing about anything. In an effective scene, when a monk, making the rounds of the imperial table to collect alms, has his face slapped by the tsar, only to say, »That was for me, now what have you to give the poor?« a violin plays a composition of mine. With one exception, every detail, scenery, paintings, sculptures, costumes, story, photography, every gesture by a player was dominated by me. But that one exception, a flash of a short scene measuring about ten feet, proved to be the straw that broke the camel's back.

That one exception turned out to be the incubator of a devastating condemnation. This short scene showed an enormous number of Russians swarming through the streets to hail the birth of a male heir to the throne of Russia. The crowd scene was not mine but came from Ernst Lubitsch's *The Patriot*, and had been woven so skillfully into the dissolves of my scenes that it was thought that I had indulged in wasteful extravagance by using such large numbers of players for so short a scene. And Mr. Lubitsch, not recognizing his own work, charged me with willful waste and disregard of costs, a charge that echoed and reechoed, never to stop. In defense of this able director, it should be said that I was too amused to enlighten him or anyone else. At the time, he was production chief of the company which employed me, and held himself responsible for the work of other directors. This, of course, helps to impair a man's eyesight.

It is possible that I was too extravagant, but never with the cost of a film. Not only had I begun my directorial career with the least expensive feature film on record but I took no pride in any waste, and permitted none, wasting nothing but myself. One detail of this film which escaped notice was that the reverberating roar of the Kremlin bells, which the tsars used to clang with the heads of those they disliked, was produced by slowing down and distorting the tinkle of a small silver dinner bell. The deafening sounds of the giant bells were not recorded by taking crew and machinery to the top of Westminster Abbey.

And while producers and directors were standing in line waiting for me to unhand an actress so that they might show what could really be accomplished with her, I had one more opportunity to affront the many friends I had made for her.

My last and most unpopular film of this series was based on a book by Pierre Louÿs; John Dos Passos, in bed with undulant fever, was trying to help in writing the adaptation. With the dice loaded so that I could not win, I paid a final tribute to the lady I had seen lean against the wings of a Berlin stage, at the same time planning an affectionate salute to Spain and its traditions. As if I were a computing machine, I built scene after scene to form an exact pattern, allowing nothing but the future audience to escape my attention, and adding to my normal duties the task of handling the camera mechanism. The intention was to call the film *Capriccio Espagnol*. This was negated by Mr. Lubitsch, in full charge of the studio, and though he was unable to interfere with my production, he set his seal on it by altering the title to *The Devil Is a Woman*. This accent is not mine. Though Mr. Lubitsch's poetic intention to suggest altering the sex of the devil was meant to aid in selling the picture, it did not do so.

The film was banned by the Spanish government, which, in turn, was banned by Generalissimo Franco, but not before its diplomats made protestations to our government that caused the work to be withdrawn from circulation. The ostensible reason given was that the Guárdia Civil had been shown to be ineffectual in curbing a riotous carnival during which the action of the film takes place. The film, shown only at the Museum of Modern Art in New York until it was shipped to Venice in 1959 for participation at its film festival, was again put into limited circulation in 1961. Curiously enough, that year witnessed another temporary banning of a film by the Spanish government, this time *Viridiana*, made by one of the ablest directors, Luis Buñuel, and a credit to Spain, where it was filmed.

But before my salute to the Spanish people was withdrawn, my work as an artist had gained a more or less profound recognition, as this quotation from a contemporary magazine testifies: »An electrician was rearranging a heavy lamp above the set. In moving around, he dislodged a large coil of rope which fell and hit the stage with a resounding thud. As a nimble-footed extra sidestepped the impact in time, he shouted: ›Hey you, be careful! I ain't von Sternberg.‹« (*Modern Screen*, February, 1935).

There are some minor details in connection with

this film that escaped the attention of the fourth estate, ordinarily so vigilant at that time about my faibles. One of my assistants, a most able one, was Mr. Rudolf Sieber, husband of the leading lady. And I no longer sported a walking stick, which had aroused so much antagonism, but instead carried a spray gun and a rifle.

The spray gun was used to cover greens and all dark spots with aluminum to save time, as it was quicker to spray light than to use electric fixtures to photograph dark surfaces. The air rifle was employed to pop toy balloons, which were released to float away into the air after every scene.

Though it was soon evident that the aluminum spray gun cut the lighting time in half, no one was able to arrive at why I guided the movements of the camera with my left hand, while my right hand held a rifle which ripped a toy balloon to signal the end of each scene.

This mysterious behavior, not in the tradition and pomp of my profession, aroused no one's anger so much as that of my leading lady. The few who have seen this film might recall how my Concha, for so Marlene was named in the film, first appears in the turmoil of the carnival. Her face concealed by swaying toy balloons, she stands in a horse-drawn carriage, making its way through a masked and boisterous crowd of revelers. The scene shows a sling used by one of the masked men who wishes to attract her attention.

When Marlene arrived on the stage to have this action explained to her, she suddenly realized why I had indulged in what was thought to be an idle whim. Neither of us would have permitted anyone else to shoot a pellet from a rifle at the wavering target of her covered face. When the scene began, I took aim and exploded the concealing balloons to reveal one of the most fearless and charming countenances in the history of films. Not a quiver of an eyelash, nor the slightest twitch in the wide gleaming smile was recorded by the camera at a time when anyone other than this extraordinary woman would have trembled in fear.

With the completion of this last film with her, an insistent demand came from all over the globe that this creature I had ruined be torn from my iron clasp. My clasp had been quite loose, and »ruin« was hardly the word to describe what had been done with her. When we first met, her pay was lower than that of a bricklayer, and had she remained where she was, she might have had to endure the fate of a Germany under Hitler.

I was told that during the many films made after my »fiasco« with her she would often go through a scene and finish it by whispering through the microphone, »Where are you, Jo?« Well, I'm right here, and should she be angry once more, when she reads this, she might recall that she was often angry with me, and for no good reason.

My next step after completing this assignment was to take a plane for Havana. Though there was one of the numerous revolutions, it failed to bother me. It was pleasant to walk alone. I had ended a period of servitude which at least had brought no discredit to anyone but me.

PHOTO CREDITS

122 © by Harry Croner, Berlin; 6, 12, 19, 45, 58, 65a, 90a, 95, 97, 105 © by Stiftung Deutscher Kinemathek, Berlin; 27 © 1984 by Dr. Konrad Karkosch, Munich; 123 © 1984 by the Estate of Herbert List with kind permission of Max Scheler, Hamburg; 118 © 1960 by Harald Meisert, Frankfurt; 88 © 1982 by George Hurrell/Sygma, with kind permission of the Panids Presseagentur GmbH, Munich; 7, 11, 43, 73 private collection, Munich; 121 © 1984 by the Estate of Liselotte Strelow, with kind permission of the Rheinisches Landesmuseum, Bonn; 5, 10 © 1984 by Ullstein Bilderdienst, Berlin; 40 © 1984 with kind permission of the Henschel Verlag, Berlin, German Democratic Republic; 108 © 1950 by Erwin Blumenfeld, with kind permission of Kathleen Blumenfeld, Gif-sur-Yvette; 119 © 1959 by François Gragnon; 1, 4, 9, 13–18, 20–26, 28–39, 41, 42, 44, 46, 47, 49–57, 59–64, 65, 67–72, 74, 80–86, 89, 90, 91, 96, 98, 99, 103, 104, 106, 107, 117, 120 © 1984 by Kobal Collection, London; 116 © 1955 by Norman Parkinson, London; 115 © 1955 by A. Armstrong-Jones, Lord Snowdon, with kind permission of Camera Press Ltd., London; 48, 76–78 © 1984 Cecil Beaton Photographs, with kind permission of Sotheby's Belgravia, London; 2, 3 © 1927 by d'Ora Bender, with kind permission of the Bild-Archiv of the Österreichische Nationalbibliothek, Vienna; 114 © 1955 by Richard Avedon, New York; 66 © 1984 by the Estate of Anton Bruehl, with kind permission of Anton Bruehl, Jr., San Francisco; 111 © 1948 by Condé Nast Publications, Inc., New York, with kind permission of Irving Penn; 87 © 1982 by George Hurrell, with kind permission of Creative Art Images, Encino, California; 93 © 1984 by Culver Pictures, Inc., New York; 92 © 1940 by Nikolas Muray, with kind permission of The International Museum of Photography at the George Eastman House, Rochester, New York; 110 © 1984 by the Estate of John Engstead, with kind permission of Franciene Watkins, Los Angeles; 112, 113 © 1952 by Milton H. Greene, Los Angeles; 100–102, 109 © 1942 by Horst P. Horst, New York; 79 © 1984 by the Estate of George Hoyningen-Huene, with kind permission of Horst P. Horst, New York; 75, 94 © 1984 with kind permission of the Museum of Modern Art, Film Stills Archive, New York; 8 © 1929 by Alfred Eisenstaedt, LIFE Magazine, New York.